I AIN'T MAD AT YA

A Black British Experience

Owen Broomfield

tangent
books

I Ain't Mad At Ya

First published 2017 by Tangent Books
& Reggae Archive Records

Tangent Books
Unit 5.16 Paintworks
Bristol
BS4 3EH
0117 972 0645
tangentbooks.co.uk
richard@tangentbooks.co.uk

Reggae Archive Records
C/o Crystal WM, 19 Portland Square, Bristol BS2 8SJ
07885 498 402
reggaearchiverecords.com
info@reggaearchiverecords.com

ISBN 978-1-910089-59-0

Author: Owen Broomfield

Design: Nicholas Darby

Copyright: Owen Broomfield/Tangent Books/Reggae Archive Records

A CIP record of this book is available at the British Library.

Printed in the UK using paper from a sustainable source.

DEDICATION
&
THANKS

This book is dedicated to my children Nathan, Ben RIP, Aaron and my two African Princesses Safiya and Keturah. You are my world and I love you all so much. I hope that one day this book will help you to understand better who your father once was and that it will one day provide the breadcrumbs you will need to find your way home to us.

Thank you to those who took the time to talk to me about long lost memories and experiences from the past and took part in the journey of rediscovery with me so that the story could be heard one more time. For some, it was hard, uncomfortable, even painful and wasn't the normal dialogue that would take place between us. I hope that you will be able to get some joy from the recollection of memories and can take some enjoyment from the unfolding events as you read them.

Most importantly, I wish to thank all those who encouraged and supported me in writing and proofing this work. I thank you for your patience.

CONTENTS _____

PREFACE

I have written this account so that one day those who choose to, may come to know about the Jamaican people who arrived here in the Windrush era and that my own family will one day know.

I have recently found out that some things are virtually unbearable to some people in our communities. Quite simply, a lot of our people can't handle the truth. Therefore, if I have written something which may be outside your realm of understanding, please embark on your own journey of research to enable you to gain knowledge and understanding. Remember, the truth may hurt but it is not a sin.

For me, I searched for God and found myself, searched for myself and found my people and my home. Jamaica is the legacy of those who were before me. Jamaicans are the most beautiful people in the world. Hugh Masekela once said:

"In Jamaica there is sort of a spiritual ancestral ambience in the environment, where you feel a sense of the past, the African-ness of it all, and is one of the places where the African spirit lives on forever."

Even Dr Martin Luther King Junior said that he had never felt more at home anywhere else in the world adding: *"In Jamaica I feel like a human being."* He said he was proud to be among his "brothers and sisters on this wonderful island." Of Marcus Garvey, a hero for Jamaicans, Dr King also said:

"He gave Negroes in the US a sense of dignity, a sense

of personhood, a sense of manhood and self-worth."

This account starts with the journey of two strangers who arrived in the UK sometime in the 1950's to an unwelcome Birmingham. It shows how they and family members sought to build a life together in Aston and how they culturally enriched their children by sharing history, culture, customs, values, and beliefs which shaped their lives.

I am one of their children and **'I Ain't Mad at Ya'**, covers my journey up until 1983 beginning with childhood and through my most formative years growing up, remembering the friends met and lost along the way in Aston, Birmingham, UK. It is a story of how the Caribbean rhythms heard throughout my life cultivated and nurtured my love of music. This deep inherent love of music inspired me, encouraging my creative juices to flow, leading me to join a band and to follow my dream, culminating in performing in front of a Prince and winning a record deal. This period of my life has been a journey of revelations, fighting adversity and many struggles. Some of you will laugh and others may cry, but you will all be intrigued by this fascinating look at life in Aston and the record playlists predominantly listened to in each period of my journey.

Owen Broomfield

HARD LIFE IN ASTON

Jamaica, Migration, Music & the UK Community

"By the river of Babylon where we sat down and where we said we remembered Zion." - A Negro Spiritual song.

Contrary to popular belief, Jamaican people did not make the decision to come to England lightly. They responded to the British advertisements in newspapers circulated over the Island inviting people to come and work in Britain's industries and help in the process of rebuilding war ravaged Britain.

In Jamaica, the drums of welcome were still beating loudly 'come on over' which resounded around the small island in the sun. Hundreds of families from regions in Jamaica pooled together and embarked on an adventure of a lifetime, to start a new life here. Later on, others came along through 'chain' migration, joining relatives and friends who had already settled. By the time many arrived in the country of their dreams, the famous UK, the pendulum had swung and the welcome which had been extended to the Jamaican soldiers and their families had begun to turn to a more hostile one. During these post war years, they were set adrift on a sea of circumstance and it was common practice for landlords to post *'No Irish'*, *'No Blacks'*, but *'Dogs Welcome'* signs in the front window of the letting houses. In London many Jamaicans were forced to live in the subway stations because no housing provision had been organised for them on arrival. Many set out across the country to join friends and family in other towns and cities.

Regardless of the initial issues, many a course had been set and for those already here, the outlook was: *"If it falls to our luck to be streetsweepers, sweep the streets, like Raphael painted pictures, like Michaelangelo carved marble, like Shakespeare wrote poetry, and like Beethoven composed music. Sweep the streets so well that all the hosts of heaven and earth would have to pause and say. Here lived a great street sweeper."* Rev. Dr Martin Luther King Junior, June 20, 1965, Kingston, Jamaica.

Smile for me Jamaica

My formal name is Owen and my pet name is Paul. The name Owen only became known to me after I started infant school, but even then most people knew me as Paul. Why Jamaicans give a formal name at birth and then call you by a pet name has always baffled me. I've grown up being called Paul whilst my brother Charles, is called Lewis. As a consequence, it is possible to know someone all their life but not know their proper name.

My mother, Gladys Broomfield, is commonly

known as 'Miss G'. My mum has a healthy, cool, dark, smooth skin complexion – the ultimate African look. She wears glasses and behind them, her eyes show many things: strength, sadness, knowledge and wisdom but most of all love; as the saying goes, *'the eyes are the gateway to the soul'*, and her soul is truly beautiful. She is slim and petite, which fools people, as in reality she is as strong as an Ox in both body and mind.

So at about the same time Rosa Parks was sitting down on a bus in America my mum was crossing the Atlantic, free but on her way here to England. One of my mum's favourite saying is *"Paul you will never know the 'value of a mother' until me gone."*

Presumably, she still regrets leaving her mother's side as her mother died quite suddenly after her departure. She said to me *"Me come de Friday and de telegram come de following Saturday say me mother dead."* Clearly, my mum still agonises about it. My mum's siblings told her how when she left Jamaica, my grandmother's heart was broken and as a result, she died. Apparently, my grandmother worried constantly about my mum's health and did not cope with her departure to the UK.

Mum describes herself as being a very sickly child under the constant supervision of her mother. Living in Kingston throughout the week, she journeyed home to the country every weekend to see her mother and siblings. She would tell me, *"Dem always ask me why me nuh stop a town? But I couldn't stay away from my mother too tuff."*

Aunt Lee, my mum's older sister, would go to town to help care for their mother, my grandmother. Aunt Lee eventually moved to town due to her own bout of illness and as my mum said *"when she got better she get Courtney."* Courtney, together with Byjah, are my cousins.

My mother always talks about Jamaica back in her day with greatest pride telling me; *"de sea was full a boat and ship. De market and whole place busy and plenty a man have labouring job and people have to dress proper, dem time deh and when people a go a road dem wear dem straw hat like trilby hat. All de business people dem dress up smart an everywhere was busy. Even though Jamaica did poor, there was electricity and water and de people dem did try live good dem time".*

She still maintains today, as she says in her own words: *"Me never want fe come a England you-nuh. One day Miss Mary meet me inna downtown Kingston. Dem time deh, Miss Mary live a country still. Anyway, we left and go uppa Crossroad fe buy Pattie and then Mary stop upah Orange Street where one of her friends have a dress shop."*

Mummy continued: *"Every minute me see the woman a look out de window at me and a smile. Dat time Mary must have tell de woman say she have ticket for me. Anyway, then we left and go a Parade. Parade a where we catch bus dem and that's when Mary gives me the ticket'.* Mummy continued *"...dem time de we used to hear how England stay."* I asked her *"wha you mean? "* She responded *"England did cold in dem days Paul." "Dem time deh, everybody get a five year passport. Some couldn't tek de cold and go back. But some nuh go back."*

The first of the Richards clan who embarked on a life changing journey to live in England in the fridge, were Uncle Sam and Aunt May. They arrived in 1953, and lived together in a house on Reservoir Road, Edgbaston where my mum joined them in 1955. My mum said, *"One woman did have the yard"* meaning a landlady. Unfortunately, they clashed instantly and my mum went on to say, *"that lady was a facety woman"*, she had complained that mummy had come and broken up her happy family setting. Mum questioned the landlady and said *"Wait ya, a-which family you have in ya? A Fe-me blood family?"* She said they all upped and moved out of that woman's house and moved to a house on Barker Street, Handsworth. Following that they moved to Waterwork Street, Aston, and then into 'Busha's' House on Upper Sutton Street, Aston. My mum was still a single woman so I asked her how she met the old man, and she explained *"Me friend dem tell me bout him, an den bring him come."*

Mr Bedda is my dad, aka 'B' as my mum called him; his real name is *Hartnel Dormay Broomfield* and he came from St Elizabeth, one of Jamaica's largest parishes, located on the southwest of the island. My dad was approximately 5'11" tall, toned and extremely popular. His appearance and complexion were similar to that of Michael Manley, one of Jamaica's Prime Ministers.

He existed like a ghost and there was never any discussion about the family back home (Jamaica). He was a closed book and never answered questions which were posed to him. It would have been easier to start back in Africa and work up to the present day than get information about one generation back.

My paternal grandmother, Agatha Ebanks, was the daughter of a Charles Ebanks. My grandfather was called David Broomfield. Whilst there are a lot of families with these names, it is certain that these people actually existed at the turn of the 1900's in St Elizabeth Jamaica. Genealogy records indicate that they married in 1925, and a Hartnel Dormay Broomfield was born to them and is recorded on the register as their son. This would mean my dad was born in 1926 and Evangeline Broomfield was born in 1929, who I assume is my late Aunt Iris.

In the 1920's, Cuba had a seasonal sugar cane harvest which attracted Jamaicans seeking better wages than they could find at home. Thousands of Jamaicans travelled to Cuba to labour in the agricultural industry or to occupy niches in the service industry. So, it is possible that the real story behind the life-long mystery of the Broomfields is that my grandparents went to Cuba to work and died there. My dad and his sister were sent back to Jamaica and raised by relatives. Apparently, our real family name is Lewis and the Broomfield name is that of the surrogate family. This story is consistent with what my Aunt Iris, my dad's sister, told me when I was about 21 years old. She started talking to me, whilst visiting me in hospital after the first of my numerous knee surgeries, and opened up about the family's past in Jamaica. I was totally surprised to hear this new information, as it was contrary to what I had previously been told. This subsequently led me to ask my dad about it; he 'flipped', strenuously denying it all. But why would my aunt invent such a story? Why did he deny something that was so trivial in the greater scheme of things?

The politics of the day made it difficult to get passports, particularly for people who lived in Cuba as by now it was under a world trade embargo initiated by America. Maybe some of the stigma and a residue of fear lingered in the minds of my father's generation. Maybe his dislike or fear of the police was due to this or some other bad experience at their hands in his past. I told myself that maybe one day he would explain everything to me and all will be made clear.

Mummy continued *"Lard sah, England rough in dem days, when we had to rent people house they would always tek advantage."* She said *"poor B,"* through *him can't stand dirt he always ended up cleaning the house".* My dad had an obsession with cleanliness and everything had to be spotless. Mummy said that one day she came home and lots of people were in the house playing dominoes. As she entered, she could see the house was untidy, so she knew my dad was not there. She said, *"then me hear that facety woman seh, 'Busha' (the woman's husband) a guh buy bucket fe you fe you clean up"*. He laughed at my fuming mum. My mum was going to explain that she had the week's rent money in her pocket, but decided to go to Mansfield Road in Aston, where she managed to rent rooms at Mr Swaby's house; this was number 3 Mansfield Road in Aston.

'Where a women rules, streams flow uphill.'
Ethiopian Proverb

It was bank holiday and everyone had planned to go out, but mum felt unwell so remained at home. Mr and Mrs Carter said that she should stay in their room, which was the front room, to enable her to throw the key down if a visitor came. My mum didn't realise that anyone else was in the house. She said: *"Mr. Swaby was a very quiet man, u-nuh"* continuing the story mum said: "There was a knock on the door and it was Mr Brown and Uncle Sam who had driven from Smethwick when they found out mum was unwell." She explains *"dem come fe look fe me. Mr Swaby go a de front door and open it. Then slam it closed inna dem face and as soon as 'B' come, me tell him what Swaby do."*

My dad, who was a very determined and progressive man, challenged the landlord, Mr Swaby, and asked him what happened. My mum said, *"all Mr Swaby seh was him don't remember doing it because him head was hurting him."* Continuing with the story Mummy said *"'B' go up de road and come back with the leased title deeds to 9 Mansfield Road."* Shortly after this, Uncle Berty, Aunt Raslin, and then Ferdie followed suit and came to the UK and lived with them at Mansfield Road. I asked her how many people lived in the house and she replied *"dem times Paul people come and settle till they got their pardoner draw then they would get their own house."*

Life in Aston

In Britain racism was deeply entrenched at all levels of society and Jamaican families were combating racism on a daily basis. There simply was no access to housing, public services or banking but despite these early difficulties, they quickly organised themselves and created systems to enable them to move forward.

The priority for black people was to get a roof over their head, normally by renting a bed in a shared room and obtaining work before the small amount of savings dissipated. Finding work or a means to generate income was a fundamental aspect of survival as the income would be used to support the family back home in Jamaica as well as rental, food and fuel costs. Residual income would be paid into a 'pardoner.'

A 'pardoner' is basically a system where a number of people put an agreed sum of money into a pot. Each week one of the members would receive the total pot, less banker costs which were normally about 1%. This system was the primary process used by many Jamaicans to harness spending power to enable them to have purchasing power. A 'pardoner' draw would occasionally be used as a deposit towards the cost of a house allowing the process of chain migration to occur.

The makeup of the household living at Mansfield Road was an ever changing dynamic as family members arrived from Jamaica. The fresh sounds, in terms of spoken dialect of patois, and the sweet smells of Jamaican cooking all around us. The traditional picture of white Jesus on the wall was a norm in every Caribbean household and a picture with words from the Bible that reads:

'Christ is the head of this house, the unseen guest at every meal, the silent listener to every conversation'

In our house we also had a gold plaque with the Lord's Prayer written on it, and another with Psalm 23:

'The Lord is my Shepherd, I shall not want
he maketh me to lie down in green pastures he
leadeth me beside the still waters'

I suppose these migrants had a lot to pray for and in time, a lot to be thankful for.

Small Miracles

At the time when a young Cassius Clay won an

Olympic gold medal for boxing, my 41 year old mum won her own two gold medals - her first child; a son Charles and in 1962, I was born. Five years later, my sister was born and my mum had her last medal, a daughter.

I am Aston born and bred. As opposed to my brother and sister who were born at Dudley Road hospital in Edgbaston, my mum gave birth to me at 9 Mansfield. She said that, *"one Saturday when me pregnant with you, I was just goin' downstairs to get a drink of water and you come before me get de drink."* She always said that when my brother and sister started walking, they would go to her with outstretched arms. I on the other hand took my first steps toward the open front door.

A lot of pressure was placed on mothers from migrant families to return to work in order to make ends meet. Therefore, it was common place for couples to leave their children in the care of babysitters, which enabled them to re-join the workforce relatively quickly.

Originally, Mrs Whittaker looked after us, that is, my brother, cousin Gay and I. One afternoon, my mum went to collect us from Mrs Whittaker's house on Whitehead Road. She knocked on the door but nobody answered so alarm bells started to ring. Becoming anxious, she stepped backwards and looked upstairs, to see if anyone was looking through the window. As she stepped backwards, she saw me coming down the road towards her. I walked up to her and said *"Miss Whittaker lick* (meaning slapped) *Cousin Gay in her head"* She kept repeating it over again and laughing to herself. *"That Miss Whittaker lick Gay in her head"* over and over again and laughing. She clearly enjoyed that memory, as I have never heard her laugh so much when recounting any of her numerous tales. My mum went on and said *"that's the reason that your dad started workin' nights, so that he could look after unuh"*, meaning us kids until she came home from work.

One of my mum's greatest skills is the way she took great care of us when we were ill. She made a variety of home remedies to care of the minor illnesses we had has children.

Tala Wappie's House - Early Music Scene

The constant aggression by white gangs in pubs and clubs of the day forced black entrepreneurialism that directly led to the advent of the 'Blues' party. The 'Blues' became a means of generating regular and substantial income. The emergence of the uniquely Jamaican phenomenon the 'sound system' was exported with the Jamaicans to the UK. This was basically a street disco-tech where people danced until they dropped. At the same time in Jamaica, armed and dangerous gangs known as the 'Rude Boys' controlled Kingston and began to force record producers to make Ska music specifically for them. However, a new sound called Rock Steady emerged and became Jamaica's first pop music genre replacing instrumental Ska and Rude Boy music. Producers quickly realised that the ghetto produced more singers than middle class Jamaica.

Many overseas farm workers realised they could make money by selling records that they had purchased abroad, back to the 'Sound Systems' themselves in Jamaica. Soon sound systems replaced the bandstand musicians in Jamaica and the sound started to take over. Before Jamaican Independence, most of the entertainment was provided by Jamaican bands mostly imitating American R'n'B music. The band music evolved into Jamaica's own Ska music genre and encouraged new independent Jamaicans to go out, dance and spend money over the bar. Sound system owners soon realised that the discotheque music coupled with strong rum called 'Rude', made them a lot of money each night.

My parents' house on Mansfield Road was right next door to Mansfield Road 'blues' and every weekend, our neighbour Stanley, known as 'Tala Wappie', cranked up his sound system to blow out the sweet sounds of Jamaica. Jamaican men worked hard during the week and the blues provided an outlet, that vital spark that re-energised the individual for another week of toil in the dirty crusty factories of Aston.

Tala Wappie had three children, Cherry, Dennis, and Jennifer. Dennis was about ten years my senior and was a proper 'rude-bwoy'. Cherry was the oldest of the three and was a godly soul, always playing the mum role and taking the time to make sure we were okay and happy. She knew everything and always looked out for us and spoke in a soft reassuring voice. Jennifer was the youngest, and as she was the same age as me we always spent a lot of time together; like brother and sister. Stanley started work very early and Jennifer would come over to our house before my mum left for work at 5.00 a.m.

I spent many nights hanging out of the back bedroom window, antagonising the elders in the garden who were chatting, blazing Ganja and having drunken conversations. The crashing sound of dominoes being slammed on tables and the joyous shouting and laughter above the music could be heard coming from the patrons. I clearly recall the aromatic fragrances of alcohol and weed filling my bedroom through the open window on summer nights.

My mum had great pleasure in telling me a story about my mischievousness as a child. She told me that a man came to Mansfield Road looking for Stanley aka 'Tala Wappie'. The man was already standing outside Stanley's gate but, he wasn't sure if he was at the right house. Standing on patrol by my front gate, the man saw me and asked if I knew where Stanley lived? My mum started chuckling to herself as she said that I told the man *"You want to know? You have to pay!"* The man had to give me two shillings. Still chuckling she said *"you grab de money out of him hand, then walk past the man, back to the same gate where the man was a stand up long time and go push open Stanley front door."* Laughing again, she said *"you was a facety little boy."*

Aston Work Conditions

I honestly think my mother was horrified when she saw where my dad worked. She explained to me that a telegram came for my dad saying that Mrs Wright, his sister in London, had died and my mum had to go to get my dad from work to give him the telegram. She described the formidable scene she witnessed in his workplace. She said *"they had to go down in to the furnace and tell him say me was there."* I've seen film footage of men working in industrial foundries and it sure isn't pretty. I can only imagine the conditions; the heat, the awful smell of other workers drenched in sweat coupled with the putrid smell of chemicals used and produced by the process. A place void of clean fresh air, where workers inhaled only air filled with toxic fumes, asbestos and soot and where no light ever shone except the glow of the flames from the furnace doors when they were opened and closed. My dad worked there for thirty years. How does someone cope with the transition from living life in the bright light of the sun to incarceration in a miserable factory prison in cold industrial Britain; a hellish blackness and unimaginable heat for six pounds a week? I understand that supporting two families, one home and another abroad, was the compelling reason for him to sacrifice his life in those conditions. Laden with debt through mortgage and responsibility for his families, he had little or no choice.

My dad was a hero; a very caring and sensitive man. Whenever he returned from work, at exactly 7.12am, he always whistled a merry tune and jingled his keys before opening the door to come in. As soon as he arrived, he would call out to me as he knew I would be awake. He would then make fried bread, fried eggs and tea for us, and a mug of coffee for himself, with salt no sugar. He would place it on a tray and bring it upstairs into the bedroom, then light the lamp to warm up the room. Following this, he would go to wake my brother up - my brother was not a morning person.

My dad was a great guy when he wasn't confronted by the pressure of having to go to hell and back each night. He struggled to deal with the demand of working the night shift and in my opinion this had an effect on his personality. It wasn't unique, as a lot of the neighbours worked at the same factory where dad worked. Birmingham was full of car factories and many Jamaicans found employment in the car automotive industry or ancillary factories and plants.

Number 9 Mansfield Road was part of a greater slum clearance programme which took place in Aston. There were lots of empty houses falling derelict along the street. The house was cold and damp, without insulation or running hot water. A coal fire in the main living room was the only source of heat and there was no bathroom facility;

the only toilet was outside at the rear of the house in a crude brick building which had no lighting. We grew up having to wash and bath in tin wash basins and when it was bath time, my mum would take one of the various sizes of tin basins from the cupboard and fill it with hot water from the metal kettle which was heated on top of the paraffin heater, or from the large pots heated on the cooker from the kitchen down stairs. The kitchen was the smallest room in the whole house containing a sink, a cold water pipe and a gas stove for cooking and baking.

As kids we had the benefit of using the 'potty' long past the potty training stages in order to prevent us freezing outside. The potty and the pail were essential toilet facilities for adults and children alike and as children, we didn't know any different - it was perfectly normal. The families who rented rooms in our house had to endure the same conditions. Trying to obtain heat was achieved via a number of activities and the main provider was a sacred object - the paraffin heater. This was normally placed in the middle of the room where people would instantly be attracted to the heat emanating from it, spinning around as the heat rose under their clothing. All water for bathing and washing was put into tin basins and placed on top of the paraffin heater. Dinner plates were placed on top of water filled pots to keep food warm. Coal was delivered every week and my brother and I transported bags of coal from the front of the house through to the back garden's coal store as well as going to purchase paraffin.

The dining room was always packed with people laughing and conversing, normally very loudly, with their individual personalities shining through. Along with the ritual soup on Saturday, the weekly dose of wrestling was a firm favourite and it generated a great deal of support and adulation for the wrestling stars of the day like 'Mick Mac Manus', 'Giant Haystacks', and 'Big Daddy.'

To understand how any society functions you must understand the relationship between the men and women. **Angela Davis.**

Untangling Family Ties

Literally hundreds of people from the surrounding towns of Gibraltar, Alexandra and Madras communities in St Anne's Jamaica, made the leap of faith and journeyed here to the UK. The absence of consistent names within my complicated family structure, adds to the problem of establishing clear lines along which one can trace ancestry. It may not be the same in all communities but in mine, and particularly amongst family members, there is an ever present veil of secrecy. When the time comes to share information about family trees or extended family lines, there is an instant and complete shutdown in discussion. Surely, it shouldn't hurt to tell your children the truth, about children sired with former partners. The false pretence portrayed of never having had a life before arriving in England is, and always will be, an enigma to me.

With such an abundance of people from St Anne's around me, and all seemingly from one family, there was an assumption on my part that it would be easy to distinguish between the blood family and non-family connections. To assume this was an error, as it has been far from easy to obtain the information. I have grown up with people who have created the illusion of a family with very non-specific lines which link people to one other; however, when under scrutiny, they have been apprehensive in confirming anything about anyone else.

The Richards Clan

I asked my mum why her maiden name was Walton not Richards. She replied, *"Paul, back home people dem time deh, dem nuh know nothing u-nuh, dem time when you beg somebody fe do something fe you, dem always do what dem want do. If you beg dem fe go a shop fe you, dem buy what dem wan fe buy, and same way when you beg somebody register baby a Spanish Town. When dem reach and can't member what you tell dem, den dem just put any name down."*

The remnants of my mum's lineage in Jamaica lives in Browns Town today albeit moving there recently. My mother's family are from a spot just outside Browns Town called Madras, situated in the parish of St Anne's Jamaica.

My great grandfather was a man called Mr Samuels

who was 105 years old when mum left Jamaica. His wife, my great grandmother, was Belle. My grandmother was a lady called Francis and her husband, my grandfather, was called Mr Richards. My mother claims to be one of the Richards clan.

My mum's siblings were **Uncle Sam**, whom I believe is the eldest male child. He married Miss Lena and lived in Smethwick but they did not have children. My parents had their first child when they were both in their forties and I can only imagine how hard it must have been for my mum to wait such a long time to conceive. After that it must also have been difficult for her to see her brother and his wife yearning for what she herself had waited so long for. She probably saw the pain in his eyes as he looked in the cot at a little baby boy sleeping, whilst she had her other son in her arms breast feeding him. Miss Lena's whole being longed for God's blessing and to have a baby of her very own. Mummy knew how they felt, the feeling of joy and pain, a longing for something that only a child brings. She herself had long given up on ever having a child so understood their silent yearning. My uncle and his wife were my Godparents and it couldn't have been easy for her, but my mum gifted me to my Uncle and Aunt, to be raised by them. This didn't sit well with my dad – it tore him up emotionally inside and one weekend Uncle Sam and Miss Lena, along with my parents, went to a wedding reception. At some point during the proceedings Uncle Sam and mummy noticed that I was missing. My mum started laughing and said *"when you father see you, him just tek you an go back a de yard!"* That's right, my dad realised how much he missed me and without discussing it with anyone, he swept me up in his arms and decided to take me home to Mansfield Road. He didn't care, and said *'they would have to understand'* – which they did because they were always active in my life, never missing birthdays or Christmas. I always knew them to be my Godparents and I'm happy to know that they had joy and happiness in their lives for a time through my mum's selfless act.

Aunt Lee, a tall slim woman, was a very strong matriarchal character and like my mother, always on the move. They were a 'tag team', always fussing, fixing things and cleaning. There were occasions when they would cuss people then serve up a big plate of food - they were magical together. My mother is a really friendly, funny character and she is in her element when she is with her siblings or mates and constantly telling jokes. She is one of those people who laugh at their own jokes and whilst laughing she claps her hands and her laugh gets louder. Nobody could argue them down on any point and whenever there was an argument, with the other siblings, Aunt Lee and my mum appeared to be telepathic as they bounced off one another taking it turns to launch verbal assaults on the others - my uncles often stood little chance in any argument with the duo and would back down. Maybe, that's the reason why most of the men in the family were very quiet and gentle in their manner.

She was an avid Christian who, without fail, attended Church every Sunday. Morality was high on her agenda and the behaviour and conduct of the brothers and cousins was of paramount importance as she had zero tolerance when it came to dishonesty, cheating or any bad behaviour and she never suffered fools gladly. She was aunty to our extended family in Smethwick where there are many more Walton cousins, not mentioned in this account. In my opinion, Aunt Lee was the closest to my mum and was the only person who could tell her what to do as they worked in a unique partnership, not shared by the other siblings because they were both food specialists. They were extraordinary in the kitchen and would cater, bake, organise, and provide food for thousands of people. Jamaican women know how to keep house and look after their men. They were raised to know how to fill the belly of their family with good cooking, and how to keep the home clean - my mum and Aunt Lee were extraordinary homemakers.

Aunt Lee and her husband Mr Jobson were a formidable couple who ruled the roost; they had two children, Courtney and Bev. Mr Jobson was a master tailor and his demeanour was that of a university professor. His profession was tailoring and he had a high quality tailor shop on Dudley Road in Edgbaston back in the Sixties, when making clothes was a talent.

Aunt May married Uncle E'rol. Their children are Joyce, Gay, Sonia and Debbie (Bromfield).

Aunt Miney married Uncle Lester (Hylton) and live in London near their children, Rose, Wilson and Beverley. My uncle known as **'Mass' Clarence** married Miss Mamma and lived in Erdington, with their children Michael, Carl, Maxine, Gillian and Tracey (Richards). There was also **Aunt Ras(lyn)** who married Mr Walker and lived in Edgbaston. They bore five children, Martin, Annie, Audrey, Peter and Paul. One of the younger male siblings was **Uncle Ferdie** who married Pauline and lived in Perry Barr bearing Dave and Yvonne (Richards). Finally, but certainly not the least, is the distinguished and impeccable gentleman, my **Uncle Berty**. I believe he is the youngest of the male siblings and married Innez (Sunbeam). They reside in London and have two children, Sharon and Elaine (Richards).

Two of my mum's sisters chose a different pathway and lived away from the main group that relocated to the UK. The eldest, **Aunt Mary,** is definitely the most revered by my mother. She married a politician (Wilson), and had five children: Joan aka 'Miss Jo', Monica, Sam, Ekcy, and Norman. As far as I am aware, most if not all of my aunt's children live in the US. My youngest aunt is called **Aunt Sil** who has five or six children named Raphel, Bailey, Donald and Sonny G, and another younger son. She chose not to leave Jamaica and move from St Anne's. Quite simply she refused the opportunity to join her siblings in UK because: *"Jamaica too nice to choose the life of living in a fridge rather than living* *in the sun.*"

The Pluto Shervington song, *'I Man Born Yah',* reminds me of my Aunt Sil. Being the youngest child, she watched her family leave Jamaica and go to pastures new. Jamaica is full of problems but as the record says:

"I man born yah, I nah leave yah, fe go a Canada"
"No way sah, Pot a boil yah and belly full yah,
Sweet Jamaica"

So in addition to my mum's siblings, there is an array of first cousins who also came to the UK and the majority of whom moved to Birmingham. These include Mass Allen (Richards), who married Miss Linda and had three children: Colin, Mikey 'Tuffis' and Pauline. There was also Luther (Higgins) who lived in Longbridge, Eddie (Walton) also lived in Smethwick (note the same name as my mum's maiden name), George (Brown) again lives in Smethwick, Brother Sal (Walcott), who lived in Handsworth and Rigs (Brown/Richards).

My Uncle Eddie Walton, mum's cousin, was an immaculately dressed man and always seemed more educated and sophisticated than many of the other family group. He was loud with a very distinctive laugh and was funny as hell, always dressed up to the 'nines,' similar to John Steed from the Avengers sporting the classic bowler and carrying an umbrella. Uncle Eddy was a musician, and played the organ at his church. His house was always full of fun as he had an organ and other keyboards littered around the room.

Quite early on it was clear that many of my cousins shared the same interests as me. A number of them either owned or were heavily involved in sound systems. On the other hand, there were those like myself who became more interested in performing music live.

As a whole, our wider family expanded considerably as the original arrivals and their offspring multiplied over the years. Traditionally, Jamaicans had large family groups and once they established themselves they were keen to create their own family household.

My Dad's Siblings

These relationships are more difficult to explain but my dad's purported siblings were my uncles Erol, Eddie, Fox and Cecil together with my Aunt Iris. As a child, I noticed that Uncle Eddie spelt his surname differently, i.e. **'Bromfield'**. All the Broomfields have a different spelling of the name that is, *'Broom'*, *'Bloom'* and *'Brom'*. Uncle Eddie, my dad's brother, was a quiet man and the total opposite of my Mum's cousin Uncle Eddie Walton the musician. This Uncle Eddie was very quiet, more of an observer, never the main contributor to the banter and was around from the beginning. He is the person in my life who allowed me to examine my own religious beliefs and played a key role in my decision to become a Christian and all other choices in my life made thereafter.

'Fox' was my dad's brother and my mum told me a story about him. *"Fox, he used to a tell lie all the time, saying that he'd won money."* She said that she believed *"some white men killed him at work."* 'Fox' worked on building the Spaghetti Junction at Aston and apparently, some men kept him back after work because he had bragged about winnings and they killed him to get the money. Unfortunately, it was another lie and he had told it to the wrong people. She said *"How machine can lick you off the motorway after everyone finished the shift and everything was lock down?"* They concluded it an accidental death and that he got hit by a crane which knocked him off the structure plunging him to his death. *"Mr. B had to pay to bury him here. He only had one week wages that the solicitors sent to his mother (Agatha) in Jamaica."*

Social Living is the Best

Miss Alva was mum's key 'Sistren' and they were always together. She was Jamaican with a broad country drawl and was married to Tass. Although she was not actively involved in my mum's activities, she was always there in the background sitting down and talking shop with my mum or they would jokingly criticise people behind their backs. She was so funny and there was always laughter around when she visited us with Tass who was a really pleasant man. Miss Alva and Tass had three children, Rose, Delroy and Audrey, who lived a few houses away and we shared the same fate i.e. lack of fencing and the absence of lawns. The gardens were an absolute trench town 'tenement yard' style, with high quality dust patches and the remnants of grass, scarred from the numerous footballs matches and other adventures played out in that arena. My dad said that we ruined it but that was hard to believe as nobody had a garden with a lawn. However, my dad always insisted that we cut the grass which existed between the mud patches. The fencing was classic Jamaican style with old 'corrugated zinc' panels with remnants of wood, normally used along the whole boundary of the garden, which was nailed in a haphazard way to create the boundaries of each back garden

Mrs Lyons had a hairdressing shop on Witton Road. She was a business woman and a lot more serious looking than the rest of my mum's friends. My mum told me that she nearly lost her life when Mrs Lyons was going to get married. Mrs Lyons was her employer and she learnt hairdressing skills whilst working for her. She had two sons, Glen and Colin, but she only spoke to one of her sons as she didn't really get on with the other. She asked my mum to stay at her house in Erdington. However, my mum began to feel sick after being there for hours on her own waiting for Mrs Lyons to return. By the time she did arrive, mum wanted to go home but Mrs Lyons was not happy about this. Uncle Ferdie came to collect mum to take her home and arrived with Mrs Lyons' brother. Mrs Lyon's brother started to act like an idiot showing off and bragging to Uncle Ferdie about how he planned to 'style it out' with his driving when he returned to Jamaica. It was late at night and the roads were practically empty so he began physically swerving the car from left to right in the road. Apparently, the car started sliding out of control and then smashed into a tree on the side my mum was sitting on. The car sustained serious damage and was written off but miraculously, my mum did not sustain any injuries. I believe my mother was impressed by the helpful and generous nature of white people as she said, *"A den you see white people"* as all the neighbours living alongside the crash site came out in their dressing gowns to assist.

Hustle Hard - If you can't play a part you will starve

My parents married in 1965; this was at a time when my mother was something of a super woman, certainly compared to the women of today. I am not saying this just because she is my mum, but because she worked hard doing hairdressing, making wigs, hairpieces, furniture dressing and bed linen. Then there was the baking – she baked cakes by the hundreds. Cake baking was an art form that she had mastered; she was not the average 'have a go' cake baker, she was a *Master Baker* and catered for lots of weddings receiving orders from all over the country. The smell of freshly baked cakes permeated throughout the whole house when she was baking, which was almost every day. She did everything from scratch - ground the fruit by hand and made the icing. Wedding cakes were presented on cake stands with a little white couple on top - black images weren't available in those days. Another chore of mine was going to get raisins and castor sugar from the local shop.

Difference

Jamaican communities have a type of 'class discrimination' which implies that the higher the skin-tone, i.e. the lighter the skin colour, the higher or better the class. In my opinion, the following account clearly shows that my mother did not want to have or see anything that reminded her of her own unique African-ness and subsequently, neither did she want me to align my feelings with that aspect of my being. It is incredibly hard not to notice how dark my mother's complexion is and compared with the complexion of the model in the 'Crying Boy' picture: as it was definitely someone from her own lost tribe.

It was either Christmas or my mum's birthday when my brother, sister and I were in mummy's room sitting on the bed giving her presents. Having purchased a 'Crying boy' picture, I wrapped it up and placed it with the other presents from my brother and sister. The glee on my mother's face as she opened the packages from my brother and sister was clearly visible. However, when she opened the present from me, her expression changed to one of disgust and at this point she threw the picture aside saying that she didn't want it. I was shocked to the core as a lot of time had been invested looking for the black version of the picture and I felt a sense of achievement and excitement after finally acquiring it for my mum. Obviously, I was seething with anger and as a child I wondered why she rejected my offering in such a callous manner. She could have faked liking it and accepted it along with the other gifts from my siblings. To this day, loving her as much as I do, I have never purchased another present for mum - I give her the money so she can choose whatever makes her happy.

At a young age, my cultural awareness and consciousness was apparent. My mother always tells me crazy stories and this one shows my knowledge of race and ethnicity in an innocent and childlike way.

Apparently, as a child, I was obsessed with ensuring that people wore appropriate clothing, particularly gloves. She told me that if anybody came to the house with gloves on, they would get questioned by me as to why dark people wore light gloves and light people wore black gloves. After the interrogation, I went around swapping everybody's gloves so that the black went with black, and white went with white or pale complexions.

Another significant indicator of my awakening consciousness and awareness of racial pride are the great Oscar nominated films; *'Guess Who's Coming To Dinner'* with Sydney Poitier and the legendary film *'Imitation of Life'*. In particular, *'Imitation of Life'* is a powerful timeless movie. It addresses racial identity issues in a magical way that pulls at your heart strings and is still relevant today. The most powerful moment is at the end of the film when the now deceased, saintly mother's precocious daughter arrives late and has to fight her way through the large crowds. By this time, the coffin has already been placed into the hearse and is about to leave on its final journey to an unknown destination. The daughter pulls open the hearse door and begins to weep uncontrollably in a loud anguished and pained manner over the coffin, whilst onlookers stand witness to her long overdue outpouring of regret and sorrow. At this point, the great African American songstress, Mahalia Jackson, performs a soul stirring vocal and this is the part where my mother and I always break down. The film instigated a thought process and I asked myself, are there really black people who want to be white and want to join in white privilege even denying their own mother in this pursuit?

Even as a child this was an absurd idea as my parents didn't look the same. My dad's family have a much lighter complexion than my mother's family. However, amongst family members we were all one complexion. I easily understand how we inherited a tone middling between the beautiful African-ness gifted to me by my mother and the lighter tone acquired from my father's genetics.

Notwithstanding all the questions in my mind regarding the film, it remains my all-time favourite for its gracious presentation of what people may call a sensitive issue. Anyone who watches this movie will be touched by it whether they are black or white.

Black Business Enterprise - Money and Work Relationship

Gibson Road Church owned a shop on the corner of Mansfield Road before Asians took it over. One of my regular chores was going there to buy the paraffin for the numerous paraffin heaters in the house. The shop was known as 'the Cha-cha man's shop'. The expression 'Cha-cha man shop' was an expression widely used by the early Jamaican settlers in the UK, to describe Indian people.

As a child, I learnt about the correlation between working and the ability to spend. The formulae was Effort (Chores) + time = Income (money to spend at Bull Ring Market). As such, our weekly Saturday morning chores included mopping and waxing the floor in the hallway from the front door to the dining room. Although the floor covering was Lino, we still had to polish it until it glistened and gleamed like marble. All the housework had to done and finished before the Bull Ring run with my mum as we had to be dressed and ready to help her carry the bags home. The Bullring Market was a massive indoor and outdoor market in the centre of Birmingham, selling fresh produce which was openly on display. It was fast and furious and negotiating over fish and food was commonplace. 'Food' in the Caribbean is 'hard food' like yam and green banana etc. The Saturday morning Bullring market run was like religion to the old black women. My mum still walks really fast and in those days she was merciless as we struggled with the shopping bags whilst she bolted from stall to stall; she knew everybody in there, the stallholders as well as the market goers. It seemed like black women from Birmingham met up and congregated in the Bull Ring market every Saturday morning and the norm was for Aunt Lee, my mum and her other shopping partner Edlin, who worked at the Post Office with her, to speed around the Bull Ring Market for hours.

Most of the people in my little village, 'Mansfield Road, B6, hustled hard to make ends meet and loved going to town to spend their hard earned cash. Spending cash was the safest option for them; possibly because they did not have bank accounts. So there were lots of door-to-door salesmen around, selling their products to black people. This was from both formal companies and the ordinary ghetto entrepreneur. For example, Mango season back in Jamaica meant big business for the ghetto entrepreneurs who were in England. Anyone who went back to Jamaica during Mango season would come back with a copious supply of mangos with the intention of selling them to all their family and friends. The proceeds would enable them to make back the money they had spent on their airfare.

Junior School

In 1967 I started at Prince Albert Infant and Junior School on Fredrick Road Aston. It had a predominantly Caribbean population with one or two white students. There were a couple of white families, the Bachelors from Albert Road, the Currans and the Beaumonts from Prestbury Road, a Polish family and a couple of Asian families. However, as a whole the population comprised of Caribbean children. I have quite a few vivid memories from this school and many of the people who feature in my coming years started out here - the very same spot as me. This was at a time when siblings attending the same school was commonplace. Some families had loads of kids - practically one in each year. This meant that one family's behaviour or reputation would affect the standing among peers in the school yard. Thankfully altercations were few and far between in those days.

A Lesson on Death and Disappointment

It was the day of my Uncle Fox's funeral, my dad's brother, who had allegedly been murdered building Spaghetti Junction at Aston. The whole family was attending the funeral and that morning my brother and I got dressed as usual and went off to school. We were aware that the funeral was due to take place at approximately eleven o'clock, so we planned to leave school and return home in time to attend it. I'm not sure if it was my parents' plan or just mine, but a strategy was agreed as to when and how we would leave school that day. After meeting my brother outside the classroom, we made our way out into the playground and planned to climb over the school wall in order to get home in time. My last memory is that of my brother reaching his hand down to me, trying to hoist me up onto the wall. A teacher rushed towards us as we were escaping. I tried, but couldn't get up onto the wall and this resulted in my brother leaving me behind in the grasp of the teacher. I was devastated and cried my heart out in protest at being restrained and kept in school for the duration of the day.

First Warrior Games

Dennis and Derek Curry, identical twins, were a year older than me, but that didn't really phase me. It felt very exciting being under the spotlight in a fight situation whilst the older boys jeered loudly.

Not knowing what to expect, I backed up towards the wall so that neither of the twins could get behind me. They threw the first blow and that was it, I rushed into them knocking them backwards, which made it easy for me to push through them, turn backwards and force them up against the wall. Grabbing hold of them by their shirt collars, one in each hand, I tried to lift them off their feet. Being short, stocky but very strong for my age, these twins were no match for me. Whilst pulling my arm back to deliver a blow, someone in the crowd grabbed my wrist and after releasing my hand from the other twin, another person grabbed my loose hand and thrust me into a wall and held me in a crucifix style. It was at this point that the twins struck several blows into my abdomen whilst the crowds cheered them on.

Whilst in junior school, I was of the opinion that Alan, aka 'Digger' was a 'waste man', the complete opposite of his brothers Bob, Cleveland and Spider, who were really cool guys. At the time, it was unheard of for any black child to pass their Eleven Plus exams. So when Alan passed the exam and went to King Edwards Grammar School in Aston, he became somewhat of celebrity as he was the first Jamaican boy known to me that passed - this achievement is still celebrated today. There were no real academic success stories for Caribbean families so Alan's accomplishment was celebrated by young and old.

Ghetto Training Academy

The six week summer school holiday can't be fun for a dad who works nights and has two sons. As children, expressing ourselves by shouting was a standard part of communication. As a result of the hyper behaviour, my dad would lose it completely and summons us to his room for a thrashing. He always stayed in the bedroom and told us to come in, insisting that we lock the door behind us and get the belt out of his trousers. The discerning part of me always knew what was coming next but as my brother isn't like me, he followed the instruction and would actually go and get the belt from my dad's trousers and give it to him. As you can imagine my dad would then summarily proceed to beat us. Or at least attempt to.

Being allowed to play out by myself gave me the opportunity to roam all over the place. My brethren Bobby and the Richards family lived on Witton Road. Bobby is the younger brother of the Great Britain martial arts star Sensei Richards. They had a massive pigeon coop in their back garden which seemed to have hundreds of pigeons. Mavis Jones lived across the road from The Barber shop and the 'Cha-cha man' shop on Witton Road sold the most Park Drive cigarettes to me for people in my house. *"Paul, come go a de shop now."*

Boundaries, whilst playing out, were defined by my mum. On a daily basis she would emphatically say *"Paul, nuh pass de house side"*, referring to the back-to-back house adjacent to the Gully *"an nuh-go inna-de scrap yard."* So, naturally I had to go into the scrap yard.

My memories of the scrap yard adventures consisted of running away from the Alsatian guard dogs. The problem was, things always seemed to end up in the scrap yard and somebody had to go and retrieve them. This was always a major operation as inside the scrap yard there were two big vicious dogs and their sole purpose was to eat any unauthorised visitor venturing into the yard outside of hours. The dogs were located near the main building which was some sort of garage workshop and was piled high with old scrap cars - a great adventure playground. The only problem was the dogs, but those dogs provided me with excellent training in athleticism, speed and coordination. It was simple, the challenge was always to get in, retrieve the item, normally balls, but on occasion other items would just end up over the fence.

The only time we saw white people was when they were going to the Villa games on a Saturday, singing loudly and drinking copious amounts of alcohol. On Sundays most of them would be going to the Catholic Church on the corner of Prestbury Road. The bells tolled and white folks would appear from all directions to attend the church service.

The Currans are one of the white families that I remember. They had a son named David and two daughters. David had a light blue 'fat wheeler' bike that he rode up and down the 'gully'. The 'gully' was a service entrance to the scrap yard, with garden access to our home and access to the front of the back-to-back houses at the rear of Mansfield Road. David and I had some crazy adventures together.

My first-ever crime was committed with David.

He had the idea, but together we conspired to 'tea leaf' an old bike from a neighbour's garden. It was an adult bike, a size twenty-six or twenty-seven, and I think we were six or seven at the time. It was a stupid idea and probably the reason I knew that being a good crook was not in my remit. The robbery plan was 'simples', we'd both creep into the garden, wheel the bike out, take it to my garden shed and paint it straight away so that no one would recognise the only bike in the 'gully'. 'Eyes on the prize' as they say. We successfully got the bike back to the shed where we decided to paint it and hide it. We found a tin of bright pink gloss paint along with some paint brushes and proceeded to paint the entire bike in bright pink. An hour or so later we began riding the pink bike up and down in the 'gully'. It was wicked, we had a big bike and then we were stopped!

An angry man grabbed the handle bars of the bike whilst shouting at me. We were carted off to the house where the bike came from and I thought to myself, *'this is it...the police...a beating from my parents...'* Surprisingly, this was not the case. The lady at the house subdued the angry man and they eventually agreed that we could keep the bike as it was not used anymore. All the lady said to me was *'ask first the next time'*. Of course my mum went along to verify they had given me the bike and they did not snitch on us. The kindness and generosity of that white couple towards me will never be forgotten. Following this incident, riding big bikes became my second sport.

The first church we attended was Six-Ways Methodist Church. A van went into the community to collect all the children and drop them back home. A few parents started to attend the church on the basis that they were encouraged and coerced by the van man. The Methodist church was big, cold and the music was rubbish. The Vicar was an old white man but the congregation were primarily Caribbean. The whole vibe was totally boring and for me, the best part was the van ride.

Organised Holiday Activities

During the six week holidays at junior school, my dad took us to Saturday morning cinema at Six Ways. This was when the original Flash Gordon and Tarzan were all the rage. The Cinema was demolished when the construction of Newtown started in the 70's.

One day, my brother and I heard loud noises. We rushed outside and saw a convoy of lorries and loads of people walking by. They were going to run a project on the bomb peck at the top of the road. Within days, youths from all over Witton, Albert, Fredrick, Dolman, Ettington, Prestbury and Grange Roads were out there hammering and building up the Batman themed adventure playground.

The Grape Vine

In those days, when my mum wanted me she would send a message via one of the boys playing outside. How she managed to track me down, I'll never know but the message always seemed to reach me eventually.

If I was late, which was my usual routine, the beating process would begin. All the way home I would be trying to think of a story that would work and prevent the beating that night. After lifting the catch to open the back door and slowly pushing my way into the dark Kitchen, my mum would bark out *"Paul? Me a go kill you ......, but come eat something first."* I've often wondered to myself 'why does she do that?', that is always feed me first and then give me a beating. I finally realised that the whole 'beating' process was basically a conversation technique extensively used by Caribbean parents as an expression of love and care. A 'beating' is normally preceded by a set of promises using words like *"I gwain bust you ass."* I'm sure Caribbean people view beating their child as a 'right' as in my opinion, it is only administered when a child misbehaves i.e. starts to answer them back, make comments or voice opinions.

The Fine Art of Beatings

Administering a good beating was like a cardio workout at the gym which sometimes left the parent out of breath, physically exhausted and sweaty. It was mostly viewed that the father's role was to be the disciplinarian which was considered a good thing for a child. In all honesty, some mothers were equally as brutal as fathers and there was no difference in the end for a child.

From the start every black child learns about the rules relating to what activity or actions will earn a beating from parents. Beatings are viewed as the answer to any disciplinary issues and were always delivered with true vigour. There were a variety of methods applied in delivering a good beating. For example some parents only used their hands to slap a child for a while. That could evolve to hitting the child with one of a selection of implements suitable for maximum effect such as leather belts, plastic belts, shoes, slippers, or 'switches' broken from hedges that used to adorn British front gardens. For many parents this would be an Olympic event as they embraced corporal punishment as helping to shape the character of young people. Very rarely did parents resort to physically punching a child because often a child would be told to get the item that would be used against them. This ploy would be used in order to give them time to reflect on what they had done and understand why they were going to be punished. This could often mean physically going to a bush and selecting the instrument that is to be used on you. The walk would often take an extensive period and be accompanied by loads of crying, two columns of green snot, and lots of tears and eye rubbing, whilst you ambled towards the desired tree to get the implement of your own destruction. This would always be a slow one as it was accompanied by the executioner's scowling and cussing which intensified and became more animated with each step you took en route to the bush. Then they'd begin to lose it because of all the crying and screaming, and the gesturing would become more erratic. They would say: *"you a cry, and you nuh get nuttun yet, mik-case an come, me a go give you sup'n fe cry fa. Me a guh bruk you ass in ya today, mik-khace me seh bwoy"* accompanied by a shove in the back of the neck which would bring out even more snot and tears.

One of the many techniques deployed by parents for beating involved shouting out one word at a time with each strike, for example, **"you"** then smack, **"want"** then smack again, **"me"** smack, **"kill"** smack, **"you"** smack, and so on. Kids do crazy things trying to escape the impact of each blow. It is at this point, that the 'beating dance', would occur. The whole beating technique was skilfully administered by the parent. The parent would lead the 'dance' by holding on tightly to the child by grasping the wrist firmly with one hand and holding an instrument, a shoe, slipper, switch or whip aloft. During the dance the child would reciprocate by jumping around, trying to escape as well as grab hold of the beating implement. The 'dance' continued until the parent finished the job.

Generally, we preferred a beating from our mum

because although more severe, it would be of shorter duration and you could break free faster. However, my mum was strong, very strict and the main disciplinarian and it wasn't all that easy to get away from her.

My mother would regularly say to me, *"If you can't hear, you must feel."* This language is universal in all Caribbean families as Caribbean parental discipline was administered. This normally happens as a consequence of bad behaviour or failing to follow instruction. The use of expressions like *"me a go kill you"*, *"A me bring you in dis world, so a me a go tek yuh out"* were regularly used and are in fact terms of endearment - Jamaican style.

My own survival routine was to eat the food offered and then fake feeling sick which would allow me to use the toilet, which in those days was outside. My dad would follow me, thus it never ever worked out well for me. It took some time for me to outgrow the notion of safe places to hide. My dad always said to me *"There are two kinds of people in the world, givers and takers. The takers may eat better, but the givers sleep well, suh mi a guh give you beating suh mi cyan sleep good"*

The youth of today don't know how lucky they are and that the English outlawed this form of discipline.

Washing Clothes Jamaican Style

My mum handwashed clothes every day in a big wash basin. There were no washing machines at that time and the larger items were handwashed on wash day.

There is a fine art to wash clothes effectively and an absolute requirement when hand washing clothes is to make the 'screech' sound. For Jamaican people, the hand washing technique has been elevated to fine art status. Every woman has to master washing clothes properly which means creating the 'screeching' sound. The sound is created from the rubbing together of cloth in water and is proven to be rigorous in scrubbing out any blemishes in the clothes. Any Jamaican woman worth their weight in gold, must have the ability to wash clothes properly otherwise them 'nuh good' resulting in them being laughed at and being called a 'wutless cruff.' So, in our house mum would sit down washing all day.

When we moved to Freer Road, carrying the clothes to the 'Bag Wash' was the weekend chore for my brother and me. As youths we didn't really consider how hard it was to put food on the table and play house keeper to sports enthusiasts. I was playing a phenomenal amount of sport on a weekly basis which included football and rugby, bringing home muddy grass-stained kits in addition to a smelly basketball kit each day. Wow, until this moment I had never considered what a mammoth task that must have been for my mum to manage.

It's hard for me to stay on top of washing my kit at this age and that's with hi tech washing machines and dryers. Fortunately the bag wash was only in Birchfield Road so it wasn't too arduous a task to undertake each week. Feeling the heat on my back from the driers as my brother and I sat waiting for the clothes to dry, made this chore tolerable. Once the clothes were dry, my style was to throw the clothes straight into the bag but my brother would always take the time to fold them first.

Hair Styling Jamaican Style

I always wanted to have a Michael Jackson afro but my dad objected to long hair on men in any form. In order to hide growing our hair, we would have to 'Konk' it. 'Konking' is a process of washing and greasing the hair and sleeping with a stocking foot on your head. This made the hair appear to be lower or flat on the skull. This was the only way in which we could actually grow our hair to any length because as soon as the old man realised that we had hair of any length, he would have it shaven off.

Having spent the whole summer avoiding my father by hiding and 'konking' my hair every night so as not to allow any growth to be seen, I had the makings of a wicked Afro ready for September. As soon as the consent letter from school was delivered asking for permission to involve me in the annual school photo session, my dad's determination to scalp us doubled. He took us to the barber's shop and slaughtered my hard-earned afro. I attended school that week, vexed beyond belief and refused to have the photo taken. However, I eventually capitulated. The saying, 'a picture says a thousand words' comes to mind.

The first 'butcher barber' was on Witton Road. The barber was a very pleasant 'cha-cha' man who would do as my dad asked. The Barber shop routine was one of my father's tasks, and he always ensured he accompanied my brother and me to the barber to give him clear instructions. Normally he would just stand there, cross his arms and say *"sciffle it!"* Whenever my dad said the loathsome words, *"S.c.i.f.f.l.e. i.t. Dano"*, the feeling of dread would come over me. Oh how I feared hearing those words. We ascended to the barber's seat one by one, but the outcome would be exactly the same for both of us.

Four large swivel chairs dominated the shop and the barber had to adjust the chair, by pumping on the pedal a few times in order to lower the seat. The barber, in his broad Asian accent would say, *"Get comfortable, you not move when I cut"* as he held the shears up for me to see. After flicking the former customer's hair from his apron, he would place it over your clothing completely covering you apart from your cranium which was exposed to the henchman and the guillotine.

I knew that wriggling about in the chair was on 'pain of death', as the response from my dad would be immediate and effective as he would swoop forward and administer a slap, right in the back of the neck. *'Brrrap!'* This sound would not only resonate in my head, but also around the shop attracting everyone's attention. Everything would stop for a split second whilst the *'Brrap!'* sound echoed and heads spun round to look and laugh at what they had heard and seen. The other youths would quickly sit still for the duration, and the adults would burst into conversation about it. That short sharp *'Brrrap!'* on the back of a bald head, did the trick every time.

I always felt haircuts were a punishment and I hated going to the barbers with a passion.

Brothers from Another Mother

I have mentioned Byjah and Courtney but not really explained how or why they call my mother their mum. Byjah lived at Mansfield Road with us as at some point he lost his mother, Mrs Miller. My mum raised him as though he were her own. He was with us until probably 1971 when we moved to Freer Road. Courtney is my first cousin and he also lived with us. I believe it was because he and his mother didn't really get on. My Aunt Lee didn't take foolishness from anyone and it was always her way or the highway.

Courtney and Byjah had two close friends, one named Edley and the other one was Desmond, a table tennis player. They would always chill and play records in our dining room. 'Young, Gifted and

Black' by Bob and Marcia, was always played as it confirmed the feelings of the youth of the day. It is extremely simple now, but in those days, the only way to get a playlist would be to use a gramophone which had a long spindle in the centre of the turntable. The playlist consisted of a selection of vinyl records which were stacked onto the spindle and as one record finished, a mechanism in the gramophone would drop the next vinyl record onto the turntable from the spindle. The turntable arm then swung across, complete with the traditional coin placed on top of the needle.

Listening to the four teenage friends talk about where their destiny would take them, whilst playing the sweetest tunes, was interesting and introduced me to the social pleasures of music and the magic of Jamaican records. Many of my childhood memories at Mansfield Road have been triggered by tracks like 'I Can See Clearly Now The Rain Has Gone' by Johnny Nash. This particular track made me believe that it 'was gonna be a bright, bright, sun shiny day...with nothing but blue skies ahead'.

The friends' list was extensive, but the ones I remember most are those found in the Windrush/Popular playlist.

PLAYLIST 1

WINDRUSH BLUES/POPULAR MUSIC

WINDRUSH BLUES

The Upsetters - Rainbow Country (Dub)
IM & David With New Religion - Black Is Black
Bobby Ellis - Step Softly
The Boris Gardiner Happening - What's Happening
Val Bennett - The Russians Are Coming
Cedric Brooks - Songbird
Funktion - Dance Of The Clangers
MBV & Mudie's All Stars - Lorna's Dance (Reggae)
Jackie Mittoo - Midnight Special, You'll Never Find
Oboe - Summer Time
Jojo Bennett - Velvet Mood
Johnny Moore - Big Big Boss
Lennox Brown - O.K Corral
Lester Sterling - Afrikaan Beat
Lloyd Radway - Love Story
Mark 'Saxa' Overton - Tribute To Tommy & Roland
aka Summer Breeze
Blue Mink - Melting Pot
Tommy McCook & The Supersonics - Michelle
Prince Buster All Stars - Almost Like Being In Love
Roy Burrowes, Clifford Jordan, Charles Davis -
Jericho Jazz
Roy Richards - Another Thing
Sonny Bradshaw Seven - Curly Locks
Soul Vendors - Swing Easy

PLAYLIST 1

Sound Dimension - Full Clip
The Fugitives - The Lecture
The Instigators - Five O
The Skatalites - Garden Fence
Isaac Hayes - Theme From Shaft
Tommy McCook - Mine Eyes, West Of Parade
Tommy McCook And The Supersonics - Indian Love
Call, Comet Rock Steady, Continental, Music Is My
Occupation, Real Cool
Tony Washington - Tribute To Muhammad Ali
Michael Chung - Village Soul
Willie Lindo - Midnight
Zap Pow - Roots Man Reggae

POPULAR MUSIC

The Tennors - Ride Yu Donkey
Al & The Vibrators With The Fugitives - Move Up
Al Brown - Here I Am Baby
Big Youth - Natty Dread She Want
Niney - Blood And Fire
Carl Malcolm - No Jestering, Miss Wire Waist
Charlie Ace & Fay - Punanny
Clancy Eccles - Fattie Fattie
Lloyd And Claudette - Queen Of The World
Cynthia Richards - Mr Postman
Dandy Livingstone - What Do you Wanna Make
Those Eyes At Me For, Suzanne, Beware Of The Devil
Dave & Ansel Collins - Double Barrel
Dawn Penn - I'll Let You Go
Dennis Brown - Silhouettes

Dennis Walks - Margaret
Derrick Morgan - Seven Letters, Tougher Than Tough
Desmond Dekker - Coomyah, Pickney Gal, Baby
Come Back
Israelites - It Mek, Sabotage, 007 (Shanty Town)
The Ebony Sisters - Let Me Tell You Boy
Eddie Lovette - Sweet Sensation
Eric Donaldson - Love Of The Common People
Ernie Smith - Duppy Gunman
Fab Five - Shaving Cream
Fabulous Five Inc. - Come Back And Stay
Freddie Notes & The Rudies - Montego Bay
The Freedom Singers - Bangerang
Greyhound - Black And White
Tiger - Guilty
Harry J. All Stars - Liquidator
The Diversions - Fatty Bum Bum
Honey Boy - Sweet Cherry
Hopeton Lewis - Take It Easy
Horace Faith - Black Pearl
Hortense Ellis - Suspicious Minds
I Roy - Welding
Jackie Edwards - What's Your Name, Keep On
Running
Jackie Robinson - Warm & Tender Love
Jimmy Cliff - Hard Road To Travel, Many Rivers To
Cross, The Harder They Come, Wonderful World,
Beautiful People, You Can Get It If You Really Want
John Jones & The Now Generation - Sylvia's Mother
Johnny Nash - Cupid, Hold Me Tight, Stir It Up, Tears
On My Pillow, I Can See Clearly Now, Cream Puff

Joyce Bond - Help Me Make It Through The Night
Justin Hinds & The Dominoes - Save A Bread, Carry
Go Bring Come, Sinners
Ken Boothe - Crying Over You, Everything I Own, Now
You Can See Me Again
Ken Parker - Jimmy Brown
Laurel Aitken - Don't Stay Out Late
Laurel Aitken - It's Too Late
Lee Perry & The Sensations - Run For Cover
Lloyd Terrel - Bang Bang Lulu
Lloydie & The Lowbites - Pussy Cat
Lord Creator - Don't Stay Out Late
Max Romeo - Wet Dream, Chi-Chi-Bud, Let The
Power Fall, Pray For Me, Put Me In The Mood, Three
Blind Mice, Young Virgin
Max Romeo And Fay Bennett - Hole Under Crutches
The Maytones - Serious Love
Millie Small - My Boy Lollipop
Nicky Thomas - God Bless The Children
Nicky Thomas - Love Of The Common People
Nora Dean - Barbwire
Pat Kelly - Festival Time
Pluto - Dat
Pluto Shervington - I Man Born Ya, Ram Goat Liver,
Your Honour
Prince Buster - Shanty Town
Prince Buster & All Stars - Shaking Up Orange Street
Prince (Buster) & Fender Prince Buster's All Stars -
Baby Version
Rico - Carolina
Roy Shirley - Hold Them

Rupie Edwards - Here Comes The Sun
Cynthia Schloss - Send Me The Pillow You Dream On
The Skatalites - Simmer Down
Sophia George - Girlie Girlie
The Soul Sisters - Wreck A Buddy
Susan Cadogan - Hurt So Good
The Blues Busters - Baby Here I Am Come And Take Me
The Cables - Jamaica
The Clarendonians - Do It Right
The Jamaicans - Ba Ba Boom
The Jolly Brothers - Conscious Man
The Kingstonians - Singer Man
The Marvels - Some Day We'll Be Together
The Maytals - We Shall Overcome
The Melodians - Rivers Of Babylon
The Mighty Maytones - Madness
The Pioneers - Let Your Yeah Be Yeah, Long Shot Kick De Bucket, Time Hard
The Slickers - Johnny Too Bad
The Starlites - Soldering, Hold My Hand
The Termites - Rub Up Push Up
Tito Simon - This Monday Morning Feeling
Tony Tribe - Red Red Wine
Toots & The Maytals - Just Tell Me, Pressure Drop, 54-46 Was My Number, It Must Be True Love, Monkey Man
Winston Groovy - Please Don't Make Me Cry

2

LOVE THY NEIGHBOUR

It was in April 1971 that my dad told the family that we were moving to a new house on Freer Road in Aston. This exciting news really grabbed my attention as I knew where Freer Road was and immediately liked the idea. Freer Road, in my mind, was a proper road with nice houses unlike Mansfield Road which by now had become a sight for sore eyes as the properties were not re-occupied once they had been vacated.

After being told the news about our up-and-coming move, my brother and I became curious and felt impelled to go and explore. We went through a scrap yard situated on Fentham Road which allowed us access to Freer Road. Once we had located the house, we separated with my brother having a look inside (my uncles were already painting the outside of the house) and I toured outside as my primary interest was the garden.

The 'entry' side of the house was absolutely fascinating, a bit different to the gully access we previously had at the old house. The Freer Road house must have previously been owned by someone in the horticultural society because the garden was fabulous. I had never seen a real garden before - we saw programmes on TV but didn't actually know anyone who really looked after a garden and flower beds. Unusually, the garden had a really nice wooden fence on both sides and there were no zinc elements to be seen. There was a seven foot high brick wall at the end of the garden that led to the rear of the flats on Trinity Road. In the garden, at each end, there were two apple trees, eating apples on one and cooking apples on the other. There were roses of every colour and other flowers, topped off with a nice little shed which housed lawn mower and gardening tools. It was our little piece of England. Sharing a bedroom with my brother was absolutely perfect for us.

My brother and I shared the bedroom at the front of the house. Being the older brother, his tastes dominated the room he as he had to have everything organised, even posters on the wall! Our bedroom was filled with images of Michael Jackson or the Jackson Five sporting wicked Afros. The consolation prize was that my dad didn't throw a fit when he came into the room as it was so tidy.

Our parents took the rear room looking out on to the garden and the third room was set aside for my sister who was a baby at the time.

The benefit of me having an older brother was that I often ended up doing things that I wanted to do because I had someone older to do it with and we experienced and went through a lot together. Because we are so close in age, we could be responsible for ourselves without too much undue pressure on the older brother. To be honest, most people thought I was the older one, maybe because my Jamaican dialect was so much broader than my brother's which led people to assume that I was the elder.

We were going to the shop at the bottom of the road for mummy on the day that we moved in. Some of the older and bigger guys, who lived down the road, were outside their houses chatting. It was hard not to notice that one boy in particularly was extremely loud and animated. There was a sense that something crazy was going to happen - and it did. My brother was riding his bike and I ran alongside him. As we approached the boys standing by the alleyway at the entrance to one of the houses, one of the boys uttered some words which were barely distinguishable due to his severe lisp. This guy was Keith Copeland who was approximately 5' 11" tall, had a dark complexion and a large gap between his two front teeth - he was the 'mouth of Aston'. The second of four brothers, Keith was by far the loudest and the most extrovert. His brothers were very humble and would leave Keith to be himself. Mr Copeland Senior was feared by all. He always looked serious, and the tone and volume of his voice would leave those with a frail disposition terrified. Keith was definitely his father's son.

Keith had a wire flex in his hand from an old electric iron and as we passed by, this fool whipped Lewis across his back. Not in a vicious way but any whip hurts especially when you are not expecting it. We stopped to remonstrate but we were no match for the guys so we had to carry on down the road and hold our peace. I swore that I would take revenge on that group of guys when I got older and bigger.

After the trauma of that first day assault by Keith and his crew, we quickly settled in the community getting to know all the neighbours. Before the end of the first day I was hanging out with David aka 'Skipper' who was a tall slim guy with dark brown hair and Nicholas aka 'Plug' who was lighter skinned, gangly, with really excited eyes and slightly goofy teeth. He spoke very quickly and always told jokes and laughed out loud afterwards. I was never sure which was funnier, his jokes or the sight of him laughing at them.

There were several families living on Freer Road with lots of boys who all became friends including the McCoys, Wilkinsons and the Largies, each having eight or nine siblings. The Douglas family, who are related to the Largies, lived further up the road and in the opposite direction lived the Sweeney, Copeland, Lyndsey and Matthews families. My family, along with the West and Miles families, were small in comparison.

In 1972 the Taylor family moved to Freer Road next door to the Copelands. The Copelands were a family of four, completing the line-up of families that became a part of my own story, sharing the highs, the lows and playing a major role in the adventures to come.

All the surrounding roads were exactly the same and the area was a thriving network of Jamaican families helping and supporting each other where necessary. We got fed pretty much anywhere we crashed as we all ventured in and out of each other's houses on a daily basis.

Summer Holiday Bike Fun

The summer holidays had just started, the weather was hot and I had a bike; not just any old bike but a racing bike built with my own hands. One day, whilst riding down Freer Road I noticed a pile of sand outside the McCoy's house. However, in my imagination, it wasn't just a pile of sand, it was a purpose-built ramp and for a moment, thinking that I was Evel Knievel, I rode towards the 'ramp' at speed and hit the plank squarely in the middle. Pulling hard on the handle bars made the front wheel lift up high and then the whole bike launched into the air causing me to lose control. The bike then flew out from under me, throwing me into a spin and the next thing I was flat on my back on top of the sand. There was a split second of relief before realising that the bike was about to fall down on top of me and was heading towards my face. Raising my hands to protect myself from the impact, the bike crashed into my spreadeagled body on the sand. Feeling embarrassed, I jumped to my feet and reached out to pick the bike up. It was at this point that I felt an excruciating pain in my arm. Grabbing the bike with my other hand, I walked off home with one arm slightly throbbing. I arrived home and went into the dining room and sat at the table as if nothing was wrong. My mum asked me *"what happen?"* My reply was *"nothing"* and I just sat there with my arm on the table trying not to show how much it was hurting me. It must have been 'mother's instinct', as my mum eventually again asked *"what happen to you hand?"* After explaining to her what had happened, and that my arm was hurting me, I was carted off to the hospital and my arm was in plaster for the whole six weeks.

When you're a kid a day can seem like a week and there were many occasions when the Freer Road crew would invent its own action. One of the Taylors, Errol, always preferred top of the range items which also applied to bikes. Like me, he was into racing bikes and was always on the hunt for particular bike parts. On one occasion, Errol pulled out a new crank for his bike which was massive compared to any crank I had previously seen. So being a bit of bike enthusiast myself, I instantly saw the benefits of owning such a crank. My 'bike project' had been going on for some months having reached about halfway. I had to source the parts and then raise the funds to buy each of them one by one, using my savings and any income from my paper round and after school job at 'Bill the Bandit'. I sourced each and every nut and bolt used on this particular bike. It had a super lightweight racing frame, with the best racing saddle, drop handle bars, and the best centre pull brakes system on the market at that time. Errol had had a similar bike project as mine on the go but he could not source a bicycle frame quite like mine so, he wanted my bicycle frame as badly as I wanted his crank. Even my mother advised me to forget about Errol's crank saying to me *"your eyes are bigger than your belly. You already have your bike finished but your eyes are too red."* She continued, *"him have crank but you have a beautiful bike what you, yourself take the time and mek it."* She went on *"Sake-ah"* (meaning, just because) *"Errol have bigger crank than fe you but that crank alone a nuh bike. Him can't ride crank."* She was right, as always, but red eye is red eye.

Errol knew about my project and knew about the investment I had made into my parts. He assumed that I would stop at nothing to get his crank off of him and he was right. We negotiated, and agreed to share my bike, if he put his large crank on it. However, as soon as the crank was fitted to the bike, and it was ready to ride, Errol nominated himself to test the bike and that was the last time I ever clapped eyes on it.

Daddy's Shopping Trips

In 1971 fashion had not really taken off and young black kids wore an assortment of clothing styles. For example, the Bay City Rollers styled tartan trousers with high waist bands, shirts with penny collars and the tightest, brightest tank tops. Platform shoes with 'blakies' on the heels to make the clicking sound whilst walking because if your shoes didn't click, something was wrong!

It was a big event to go and buy a suit and every year, in the first week of the holidays, my dad would round up my brother and me and take us to the Burton Shop on Lozells Road to buy the annual suit and new shoes - probably because it was wedding season, the start of the industrial shutdown and he had received holiday pay. This event was funny to me because I don't remember getting a suit I liked. My brother always seemed to get clothes that fitted him properly; I on the other hand, got clothes to grow into. As a result, he is highly fashion conscious, enjoys shopping and spends a vast amount of time looking around in shops for any given item. Unlike my brother, shopping is not one of my passions.

The last suit my dad bought me from that shop was a burgundy purple woolly suit and I hated it! But as per usual it was the only suit in the shop that could fit me and was within the budget. The suit would have to 'serve' me for the whole year and was worn for church every Sunday, for a year, despite any growing that may have taken place during the period. I began to grow exponentially and was 6' 3" by the age of thirteen and was still growing. The one thing that never seemed to change was my waist size – it was always 36 inches.

In 1973 we decided to buy a car between us. I was 12 years old, Danny and Charlie were 13 and Dennis aka 'Blackeye' was 14 years old. The car was a sports model Cortina Mark 1 1600 GT, which was black with a white bonnet. It had a sports steering wheel and the standard seat cover set, giving the interior a great look, and the exhaust had a muffler. However, the car soon started to experience problems, in fact, it was one big problem. My brother and 'Blackeye' became dismayed with the amount of physical work we had to put into the car, but Danny and I were always up to doing the work - I loved and still do the mechanical greasy stuff - a born grease monkey. Between us, we stripped and rebuilt every single bit of the car from the engine up. To be honest, it was a status symbol as none of the other boys had managed to acquire a car.

Soon after the first car adventure, my parents announced that my Uncle Sam and Miss Lena were moving back to Jamaica. There was a buzz in the family and everyone was rallying around helping them to pack and sort out their affairs. Apparently, Uncle Sam told them he was giving me his much prized car a Cortina Mark 3 2.0 litre GT. Wow, I was bowled over; this car was yellow with a black roof and the car had power - what a generous gift. Everyone knew I was driving, so there was no problem on my parents' part.

I got the car and did all the necessary cleaning and 'blinging' up the hub caps and chrome-ware. There were two car garages situated on Fentham Road, one was Mack's and the other Carnegie's. Mack was a short, greasy looking white dude with brownish/blondish coloured hair and missing front teeth. He looked unkempt and always wore the same dirty overalls day in day out. 'Carnegie's garage was at the opposite end of the road. He was a black man, very dark skinned with a big bushy beard and spoke very loudly. He looked as fit as an ox and as strong as a bull and people didn't want to get on the wrong side of him. Neither of them were particularly good mechanics but they were local and cheap. Eventually I took the car to 'Mack's garage.

'Mack' checked the car and it seemed perfect until he went into the boot which revealed an absolute nightmare. He pulled and pulled at a piece of paper he saw, and before long he completely took out the wheel arch area within the boot. He started laughing and stated that someone must have repaired the boot with paper. The body was completely rotten and both wheel arches were gone. My uncle had been the victim of an unscrupulous mechanic who had fooled him into thinking he had carried out repairs on the car. The car was a write-off and I now owned a car that had a great engine and no body. My dream was shattered and I had only driven the car the length of Freer Road. In all sincerity, Mack's discovery probably saved my life.

Following this, I found a shell for a Cortina Mk3 almost exactly the same as mine, with the opposite problem. I thought that if I purchased his shell and put my engine into it that would make my car legal. I paid about £100 for the car and then paid Mack about £500 to do the work. Of course, being young and not really knowing a lot, I totally trusted everyone. Mack got the job done and the car was working for a while before the gear box went - that was it and I just scrapped the car.

At the age of approximately 16, I bought my next car from Glen for £100 who had purchased it for about £30 from a scrap yard. It was a green Triumph Toledo and I took it to Mack who fitted twin carburettors, so that the performance would be boosted substantially. Fitting the obligatory cassette player and equaliser was mandatory, and from that point forward I was mobile. This heralded a new chapter in partying.

Glen and his brothers 'Wriggler' and 'Bear' lived directly over the road from us. One evening I was outside Plug's yard at the top of the road playing football when I heard a loud screeching sound coming from the top of the road. I turned towards the direction from which the sound was coming and saw 'Wriggler' running full pelt, at what seemed like one hundred miles per hour towards us. Immediately behind him was a Police car speeding towards us in the middle of the road. 'Wriggler' suddenly turned and ran through the open gates which led to a garden to the rear of the houses on Hampton Road and disappeared. He literally jumped over the garden fence into the neighbour's garden completely clearing six foot fencing without even touching it. By this time the police car had screeched to a halt in the middle of the road and two police officers jumped out of the car to pursue him, running towards the opening to the garden. They decided to give up as they were literally stopped in their tracks by the height of the fence. I heard one policeman say "how high did this guy just jump?"

realising there was absolutely no way they were going get over that fence. I saw 'Wriggler' jump over a six foot six inches fence without touching it, clearing it with the greatest of ease. He didn't even break his stride or use his hands. It was an unbelievable feat and even until now I can't believe how high this guy jumped. I have been back to the same spot many times and it's still just absolutely unbelievable.

Jamaica Home Coming Trip

A large number of Jamaican people who came to England settled in the Aston and Handsworth areas of Birmingham. The task of travelling back to Jamaica was an awesome one which required hours of meticulous planning and in about 1972, quite soon after we moved to Freer Road, my dad made arrangements to return home to Jamaica for the first time since he had arrived in the UK. Everyone at the house was excited as my father was going to see his family and friends back home. In those days people who went to Jamaica normally went for six weeks during main shutdown throughout the summer. At the time there were no budget airlines or quick trips to the Caribbean so it cost an absolute fortune for returnees. I remember vividly, the day my dad came back to England and returned home and I still recall the eager anticipation felt by everyone that day. We didn't know what time he was due to arrive back home, but we knew it was imminent. As usual,

I was playing outside with 'Plug' and 'Skipper'.

It was a bright sunny day, I'm not sure if one of the lads spotted him first but it was definitely him at the bottom of the road. I knew him instantly even though he seemed to be very red, beetroot red. I didn't realise that black people got a sun tan or sunburnt and the idea of black people using sun block was an unknown quantity. I raced down the hill towards him, as he was plodding up the hill towards the house carrying his two suitcases. He was positively beaming and smelt of white rum. He was not drunk, but slightly mellow and glowing. In those days there was a limitation on how much alcohol could be brought duty free. My dad was happy that day and he could see my brother and me sprinting down the road towards him. He put down his cases and opened his arms to catch us as we raced to embrace him. We hugged, laughed and asked him what he'd brought back for us. We both carried a suitcase as we walked alongside him toward the house asking him a million questions about the trip.

Arriving at the front gate, I dispensed with my carrying duties and ran in the house. My mum was in the kitchen and I shouted "daddy has come home". It was a happy moment for everyone. Of course mummy was as pleased to see him as we were and It wasn't very long before people started arriving as mum instantly got on the phone and spread the word that 'B' was home. My brother and I were fighting to get into the suitcases to see what he had bought back, for us in particular. I remember getting a straw hat and some other trinkets and beads consistent with the day. There were about twenty large bottles of Wray & Nephew 100% proof, white rum in each of the suitcases along with a lot of records. The adults brought out the 'Rum' glasses as more and more people arrived to join in the festivities. Uncle 'E'rol and Uncle Ferdie, together with Uncle Sam and Miss Lena, travelled from Smethwick and soon the whole gang turned up to see daddy talk about the trip and drink rum. My brother and I attempted to get the records out to play but daddy intervened cautioning us on how to handle his new music. We had handled records before with no complaints, but I understood that these records were fresh off the rock.

I remember one particular tune, 'Ram Goat Liver'. The records were played over and over again and everybody who came heard the latest grooves direct from yard and drank rum.

Mummy Jamaica Homecoming Version

The following year mummy was set for her return to her home. Unlike my dad's, my mum's packing was a massive task. For some strange reason my mum appeared to want to take all the food that she could purchase and expected it to fit into her suitcases. I asked my mother whether there was food in Jamaica as it was a mystery to me why she needed to take food if she was going to a place that had fresh food like bananas and yam hanging off the trees and growing freely.

My mum told me *"this kind of food is expensive in Jamaica"* and she needed to take some back with her so the *"people dem can taste a little bit of Britain."* Naturally, I asked whether she was carrying it for everybody in Jamaica because the food that she packed could never have been for one person.

Starting out in Music

The first musical instrument that became of interest to me was the piano. We had a piano whilst we were living at Mansfield Road and Daddy, Ferdie and Uncle Sam had the gruelling task of moving it to our new house on Freer Road. The three of them had to navigate it through the front door and manoeuvre it into the front room. Uncle Sam kept telling my dad to be careful so as not to hurt his back, but of course, my Pops was all man and therefore immune to sensible advice. By the time they actually got it into the room, my dad screamed out as he had hurt his back and was laid up for the next few weeks.

This is where playing a musical instrument really began to enter my thoughts in a meaningful way. My sister had begun to have piano lessons with Mr Blissett, who was a long-established piano teacher. Mr Blissett was a staunch Christian man with a large family of children, many of whom are older than me. Whenever my sister came home from her lessons, she would practice using a music book. Instantly, I was able to sit down beside her and play the whole tune using both hands on the keyboard with relative ease. I soon persuaded my mother to pay for me to attend piano lessons. My argument was easy to win because I was able to sit down and play all lessons from memory whilst my sister struggled to recall perfectly during her practice sessions. My mother contacted the teacher, and the next time my sister went, I accompanied her. I quickly played my way through the first two stages of piano lesson books. But my biggest problem was reading the music as I never really enjoyed the 'reading sheet music' element. However, once I heard a song played in its entirety, my ability to memorise music meant I could play it back straight from memory. I quickly learnt to navigate around simple chords and accompany most songs just playing the chord structure and the melodies. It wasn't too long before my brother got interested in playing an instrument and wanted to escalate to owning musical instruments.

My mum ordered two guitars from Kay's catalogue, a four-string bass and a six-string guitar along with a small amplifier on which we would practice. My brother and I then set about learning to play the guitars. After constantly playing the guitars, the guitar strings snapped so we had to purchase new strings from the only shop we knew.

Having a mother who has always encouraged me is a blessing. On many occasions she would say to me, *"Paul, you can and should do whatever you set your mind to and if you set your mind to it, you can achieve anything."* My mum scrimped and saved for me to have piano lessons and to purchase the guitars. These simple acts are proof that she had belief in me, without actually saying it and as the saying goes, 'actions speak louder than words.'

Musical Exchange Broad Street

We were allowed to go, on our own, to Musical Exchange which was situated in Birmingham city centre to purchase our first set of guitar strings. The staff, Gary and Dave, were friendly; they made us feel welcome and at ease whilst we waited our turn to see them. Gary and Dave could be seen giving their sales pitch and demonstrations to other customers and we had to wait quite a long time to be seen. When they served us, they treated us in exactly the same way as the other customers and catered to our every need. They were exceptional, and I continued to purchase musical equipment from this shop whilst in the band and after I left.

Our neighbours, 'Blackeye' and Danny started coming over to show us a few chords and occasionally brought their guitars, their dad's amplifier and speaker. We would spend many hours jamming together with them in our bedroom. They were both experienced musicians so we learned a lot from them and I picked it up relatively easily, already having gained some rudimental music knowledge from the piano lessons. 'Blackeye' was a bassist and Danny an accomplished guitarist. They both played in the band at Gibson Road Church and that was the spark, the initial reason for us wanting to go along to that church in the first place.

It was a blessing living across the road from the brothers because we were able to spend a considerable amount of time together practicing. We practiced hard, and quickly learned the basics of the guitar fretboard together with the arrangement of notes across it. We had a few formal guitar lessons, but decided that what we learnt in an hour wasn't beneficial to us; we wanted to be able to play along to all the songs that they knew. Within a few months we could tune and play the guitars well enough to accompany 'Blackeye' or Danny and it wasn't too long before my desire to play, turned into a desire to join other musicians and see how they performed on their instruments. It was not commonplace to see live music being played, so church was the best place to access live music regularly and we were able to accompany 'Blackeye' and Danny on a few church songs.

The Music at Gibson Road Church

The famous Gibson Road Church is a microcosm of Jamaica and the Caribbean as a whole.

The annual national convention was when affiliated members from all over the country, along with celebratory charismatic preachers from America or the Caribbean, came together to worship for one week. Conventions were fantastic as there was always a great vibe, and a great place for all the families to bond. The music in the church was divided by age and the keyboard players played for their respective choirs. Paulette Witton was the keyboard player for the older people's choir and the young people's choir had the Johnsons - Fitzroy and Trevor, who were keyboard maestros and undeniably brilliant. For example, whenever Fitzroy was on the organ and Trevor on piano the church was going to be 'rocking'.

Of course there were a string of other musicians alongside them: on drums was David Harris, 'Blackeye' on bass guitar and Danny on rhythm guitar. It was a very informal setup and basically, whoever had a guitar could play along. Suddenly the boring version of *Amazing Grace* sounded phenomenal. Other prominent players at church were the Burke family, Ian, Simeon and their big brothers Glen and Vernal who ran the young people's choir. They always produced a really good sound and that was all that I needed to enjoy the church service. Gibson Road church was a total contrast to the old cold church with the pipe organs which we used to attend on Witton Road. This church was vibrant and full of energy, and good-looking girls.

As teenagers, my brother and I began to get more interested and involved in church and suddenly it became easy for my mother to get us to attend on a regular basis. Dennis and Danny were now our firm friends and the fact that mummy knew a lot of people in the church helped. My Uncle, Eddie Bromfield, was a church Deacon so he was really pleased when we became members at the church. We instantly became a part of the family there. The music had such a distinctive and seducing sound and with the young people being more aligned with the American gospel sounds. The older people loved the traditional religious music from Jamaica.

It's really easy for me to now understand why some people have spent their whole lives as members of a church congregation. For some, it was the only time they would see other black people and get to communicate on a different level. I've always believed that black people need each other because whenever we get together there is always a carnival atmosphere. We are so rhythmic and passionate about music and access to it; it is as vital to the black psyche as is religion.

Baptised in Soul

My brother suddenly announced that he wanted to get baptised. This meant that he was going to become an official member of the 'church gang'. My uncle stood up at the end of the bench with his hand beckoning me to come along with my brother. I hesitated and his gestures became more animated. I asked myself "did I really want to do this?" However, by now all of the congregation were standing, singing loudly, clapping and looking at me. Somehow, I felt compelled to get up and follow my brother and walked towards my uncle's outstretched arms joining my brother and kneeling at the front of the church where lots of people were laying their hands on me and praying aloud.

Eventually we were led through to a room at the side of the church where we were each provided with a white gown, which were similar to hospital surgical gowns, and told to put them on. There were lots of enthusiastic people who were seemingly very happy with our decision to join the 'church gang'. Brother Powell and Brother Wright were in their element with joy - never had I seen Brother Wright look so happy. After getting dressed in our gowns, we were taken back into the church on the rostrum where the elders, along with the Pastor, were seated. By now the spirit was moving in the church and many people were speaking in tongues. I looked around peering at my brother through the many hands that were covering us both, and he appeared to be almost vacant . I wondered what was going through his mind but he seemed very calm and fully engrossed in the moment.

After a short while, the Bishop returned having changed his attire and we were shuffled towards a corner of the rostrum where the old people's choir normally sat. The carpets had been rolled back revealing what appeared to be a trap door in the floor which was raised up presenting a small pool filled with glistening water. Bishop went into the pool first and then we moved to the top of the stairway into the pool. Bishop beckoned, my brother first, who walked down into the rippling water and stood alongside Bishop. The water was about chest high on Bishop, we were slightly smaller but it was possible to stand up in the water. Bishop recited some words and my brother was held firmly and eased backwards into the pool until totally submerged in the water. He came up from the water, exhaled and let out a blast of water from his mouth and was born again in Jesus Christ. He was lifted up from the pool and the church became euphoric in song and dance. Having seen my brother do it, and of my own volition, I too went down into the baptism pool and arose born again in Jesus Christ. My choice, as always, was to follow my big brother.

After the church service finished everybody greeted us - people were so genuinely happy for us. All we could see were beaming smiles from everyone in the congregation. Even my Uncle Eddie had a sense of pride and stood proudly on the steps monitoring us as we greeted the gang members in the church courtyard. Everyone including 'Blackeye' and Danny were ecstatic about the baptism and we left for home to break the good news to mummy and daddy and of course murder a big plate of our traditional Sunday dinner – chicken and rice and peas - which was waiting for us. That Sunday, the food tasted even sweeter.

Great Barr School

Participating in sport, like life, is a great educational tool because it teaches that in life there are only winners and losers. You soon learn that nobody wants to be a loser and a good team can overcome any obstacle.

The first thing I learnt about myself and sport challenges at Great Barr School was that I was an absolutely diabolical cross country runner. But also learned that I had a competitive nature and soon distinguished myself in both cross country and as an all-round sportsman.

I went along to the school football trials and 'Skipper' was the only person I knew there plus we were the only black boys. The football trials were a nightmare, and following the football trials were the rugby trials. I had been attending rugby matches with my brother whilst still at junior school and already knew the teacher, the players and the rules of the game.

There was no doubt that I would start playing rugby so when the trials came, it was just a case of turning up and watching the others. With me being the fastest boy in the school and head and shoulders above the rest of the boys, when I got possession of the ball, a try was imminent, with my average score per game being sixty points. It seemed that I was physically stronger than most boys my age playing rugby and had great speed, timing and co-ordination so it was rare for other teams to score as

I would run them down before they could mount a serious challenge. The team never lost a game for the first four years.

Born to Ball

Basketball taught me that the word 'Team' means being unselfish and making others feel respected. *'There is no I in team.'*

From the very beginning there was one basketball player in particular who I single out in gratitude for introducing me to, and taking the time to teach me, the rudiments of the fine art of basketball. And that is, Richard aka 'Ricks'. He's three years older than me, but was instrumental in contributing to me picking up the gist of the game quickly. I would go to watch every game at the side of the court waiting to get to the hoop during the timeout, half time or at the end of the game.

Traditionally, the teachers chased the young fans off the court who were messing around but no one ever chased me off a court. At basketball matches 'Ricks' always tested me as well as showing me crossovers and other tricks. He told me about Michael Ewers aka 'Ibo', the basketball Guru from Broadway School. 'Ibo' had spent his early childhood years in America and therefore learnt how to play basketball. He was the local basketball 'Don' and was unstoppable; therefore Broadway's team was unstoppable.

It wasn't long before my true talents began to manifest themselves and I mastered every basketball skill imaginable - nobody could stop me from scoring. My shooting and dribbling skills became legendary amongst the older players. During away games, messing about on the court before the team came out made the opposition nervous when they watched me. My performances utterly destroyed their confidence because they could see how good I was and at that point, I wasn't in the team. That very quickly changed and I was drafted in as a starter. Thereafter I started for the three teams in the years above me and Great Barr began to get a reputation for basketball. Basketball came easy to me - if I saw it, I could do it. That included dunking, crossovers through the legs, behind the back, all the trick shots.

Great Barr School's PE teacher was a passionate basketball fanatic who ran his own basketball team which played in the West Midlands League. He had a similar appearance to the character 'Rigsby' in the sitcom Rising Damp. By the time I got in to the second year at school, now called year eight, I was eligible to play officially for the school team and the PE teacher didn't hesitate to make a team around me. We never lost a game until we came up against the mighty Broadway School and that particular game came down to the wire and Broadway School won with the last shot of the game.

Cricket Disaster

After Easter the school dropped all the regular sport and geared up for cricket and athletics season. The trials process began in the PE lesson where a series of drills and races tested students' abilities. They were then encouraged to go and play in teams that supported their skill area. I was a cricket fan. I'm a Jamaican and at the time, the West Indies cricket team was the best in the world. Being the best bowler for my age in Aston, without hesitation, I went to the cricket trials and was very excited at the prospect of playing cricket, I devastated whole teams by bowling them out for a duck and this was whilst I was at junior school. I regularly bowled adult batsmen out in the park, again for a duck. Almost instantly, I knew things weren't going to work out when I realised that the same PE teacher who had flopped me with the football team trials was conducting these trials. In my opinion, he was the perfect example of how not to motivate young people positively. In the five years at Great Barr School and having become the best all-round sportsman, I never ever had a conversation with that man. Maybe he didn't like me - well, the feeling was mutual.

In the first game the PE teacher put 'Skipper's' name down to bowl. I nearly choked as I could not believe that the teacher asked 'Skipper' to be the bowler and did not even consider putting me on the bowling rota. I was fuming as instead his plan for me was that I should patrol the boundary. I could hardly hear what was happening during the game and soon lost all interest in proceedings. At some point someone actually hit the ball and it rolled in my general direction. Now don't get me wrong here, it was not a six and the ball didn't look like it would have rolled to the boundary. However, it was coming directly towards me. Standing there with my feet astride in the traditional 'get ready to field' stance, frozen in my position and not moving my feet, I let the ball roll right up to me and allowed it to pass through my legs. Honestly, I felt insulted by him and was angry as all I could see were 'joker' bowlers.

Somewhere deep down I completely lost it and right at that moment decided that cricket wasn't for me. The teacher went crazy and after ignoring his protest, I walked off the pitch, kissing my teeth after him and that was my last cricket game ever. My view is that if there is a bowler on the team, who bowls like Courtney Walsh, and the coach does not select that bowler to play, then the coach does not deserve to have that bowler in the team! I didn't need to be there if the teacher didn't allow me to display my abilities. For me it was play or nothing - remember, this was the same teacher who also missed my potential in football.

Harlem Globetrotters

Great Barr had one positive thing going for it, and

it alone formed the centrepiece of socialisation for most of the black students: the Harlem Globetrotters trips. Each year there was an excursion to the Wembley Arena in London to watch the Harlem Globetrotters. This trip was singularly the best thing about the whole school's social experience. From the moment the music started with the whistling of Sweet Georgia Brown and when the lights in the arena went down, people began to hasten to their seats so as not to miss a moment of the famed court jesters with hilarious antics who set out to put their skills to work against daunting opposition.

The game exceeded expectations, and the spectators were as much a part of the show as the players themselves. I can still see it now, the music, the lights, the atmosphere, then the show. Girls from all years went along and dressed up to the nines and the whole school vibe was out of the window as soon as we got on the coach. People paired up and the players played. In our first year at Great Barr, Peter, 'Skipper', Louie and I were the junior stalwarts and the elders were fine women like fine wine, people like Wendy Morgan, Patsy Phillips, Carol and Janet Cummings and Marjorie Noble. Amongst the men were Ian Young, Dave Parry, Peter and Tony Francis, Michael Francis, Roy Lewis, Amos, Chrissie McBean, Ian Sawyers, Ian Grimes, Patrick Campbell, Jesse Gerald, and Keith Murrain and the list goes on. The Globetrotters experiences had an overall effect on my basketball learning and later performances.

1974 The Broadway Experience

Broadway Comprehensive School was closer to my home and finished at 4.20pm each day, which was nearly an hour later than Great Barr Comp. When I wasn't playing basketball or rugby, I would go to Broadway School on a regular basis. This happened so much that people thought I actually attended Broadway School. This still holds true today.

The experience of my regular visits to Broadway was unbelievable. Unlike my former school, people were happy and full of optimism. The school was teeming with musicians and not football hooligans. Broadway's student population was enthusiastic about going to school because all of the after-school provisions were like mini-festivals or carnival. There was always a music backdrop with dance.

The Athlete in Me

That coming year heralded the coming of the man in me; I was bigger and stronger than ever and my athletic appearances were brief, normally just a 'one take' and it was over. I did more than one event and would only take one throw then 'go-bout' my business. I don't recall having to take two throws in competition and I could throw both the javelin and the discus outrageously far. My throwing arm was strong and fast and I could virtually throw out of the stadium, certainly past the national standard in both events. To put it into context my nearest competitor was a guy called Robert Weir from Handsworth Grammar School. He was the former British Hammer thrower and twelve-time British national champion. In 1997, he competed in the World's Strongest Man competition, finishing 3rd in the final. This guy completely dwarfed me. He was absolutely 'huge' and looked as if he was chiselled from rock even back then.

At the Crossroads with Authority

It must have been summer as it was athletic season and I was 'storming' it at several athletic meetings. One day I met a girl of fine stock, a 'browning', who attended a school near Great Barr and lived in Handsworth Wood. This 'browning' became a very vocal supporter of mine during my brief appearances at athletics events. She was very mature, 'over bright' and really fancied me, so we started dating. It wasn't long before I brought her home to meet my family and it came as no surprise to me that she and my father got on like a house on fire. She fitted in straight away - this girl could talk for England.

I had little knowledge of 'street life' and had not really been involved in the effects of young black people to 'edu-taining' themselves. I was still effectively living in a bubble, that is, the bubble called church and the 'browning's' stories about going out fascinated me. She knew most of the people I knew and she had a life that sounded enthralling.

I had never attended Canterbury dances because they were normally on a night when something was going on at church and church attendance was mandatory. The church's subliminal message was that of disapproval of a Christian participating in the delights of those kinds of activities. However, the 'browning' purported to be a Christian and did not have any issues balancing regular church and regular partying. The very fact that I was a practising Christian and attended church regularly worked for her because she was also a church goer, albeit at a different church.

Her posse went to the Catholic Church which they called Chaplaincy. It seemed like a great place to meet all the nice girls at once in one spot. We, that is me and a couple of 'hungry belly' men, used to go to Chaplaincy and climb over the wall just to spend time chilling with the girls in the Chaplaincy yard. On one occasion, the 'browning' and I were messing around. Like a twat, she put her scarf around my neck, stood up on the bench above me and pulled the scarf tight, to the point where I couldn't breathe. I got into panic mode but she stopped pulling it tight just before I passed out.

The Celestial Meeting Place

One day, the 'browning' and I were out together and she told me that a man named Francis had been bothering her and coming at her hard whilst she was at Canterbury - I saw **RED!!**. By now I was 'battle hard' and had a big enough ego to tackle anyone for my new girl. In my mind, the matter had to be resolved with this Francis 'Geezer' and my intention was to track him down and confront him.

Back then, 'black music' wasn't played on the radio, so Canterbury served to provide 'edutainment' and played a big part in driving demand for record sales. In the late 1970s, the UK black youth created a musical form that was considered British called Lovers' Rock. This music was popular and offered an alternative and more focussed sensual experience for couples dancing together. As such it was a very popular element at the Canterbury functions. The dance called the 'Rub' was the preferred dance of couples when slow dancing. This dance was a physical and technical challenge largely practised in one of two forms. The traditional London 'double pump' style which our parents did and the deeper, more intense Birmingham 'single pump' style which had to be done really slow, down to the ground without thigh shakes. The problem with the Birmingham style of this dance was that the lower you dipped, the more likely it was that your thighs would shake and force you to stop dancing altogether.

The first beat of a Lovers' Rock song would play and people instantly gravitated towards finding a dancing partner. Some girls were happy to dance with pretty much anyone in the spirit of the party but the 'hungry belly men' sought to trap girls they desired. They were always more sinister and predatory young men who completely misunderstood the dance and became what we would call stalkers today. One dance could change a life for better or for worse. Most men took the dance for what it was; a dance that finished at the end of a particular record. For other men, it often caused them to become besotted with the girl they danced with which sometimes led to the beginning of a fatal attraction.

For couples bitten by the love bug, as I clearly was, Lovers' Rock said the words that we couldn't say to a woman in the dance. Some would say life was hard for a lot of people back then but we had music which offered peace, harmony and love. The whole era was very similar to the 60s flower power generation, but instead of being outside in the rain it was the era of love inside a house, dancing the 'Rub' and unconsciously erasing the velvet wallpaper off the wall (it was customary for the man to lean on the wall whilst doing the dance) and leaving the dance with cheap lipstick on collars.

My first relationship, which was with the 'browning', opened my eyes to lot of new experiences during that period of my life. One of those was learning how to 'Rub' and if I planned to go out regularly, then it meant having to face the challenge of this dance head-on. Perhaps all those years at church had left me slightly short of the experiences I would need to navigate my way through the coming challenges of life as a youth growing up in the ghetto.

I quite quickly found out that the negative outcome of the dance could essentially make you a laughing stock, particularly amongst girls. Trust me brethren, the girls wouldn't hesitate to laugh at a man in front of his squad. Worse than that was if a girl refused a man the second dance - the embarrassment can't be understated, it was considered major. The problem was that if a man was refused, then he would have to walk all the way back to where his squad was. After the refusal, it felt like everyone in the whole damn place was looking at you. You could feel eyes burning into the back of your neck and whilst taking the walk of shame, you would try to comprehend the word 'no' as it replayed in your mind. Some of the more experienced men tried to style it out by making it look as if they were just asking a woman to move out of their way so they could pass through the crowd. However, the squad always noticed the failure.

Even more soul destroying, was when a man was refused a dance and couldn't move because the party was so rammed. Another man would come along, ask the same girl for a dance and get accepted straight away. The dance would be so packed that standing there and watching another man rub down the woman that you had just asked for a dance was the only option. It was rough out there brethren, trust me.

The idea of looking for the dude called Francis was soon forgotten and thankfully our paths did not cross at Canterbury. But they would definitely cross and in the most surprising way.

England Basketball

In 1975 I was drafted to the Under 14 England basketball team and became the first student player from Great Barr School to be capped for England. Other local boys Ivor Dowdie from Broadway School and Herman Wilson from Adderley School and I were recognised for having led teams that dominated basketball at both city and regional levels for some time.

Things changed when I started playing basketball for England as I was travelling more regularly to play in national league and international matches abroad. The three of us were also drafted into the Team Fiat junior team. This was the cadet team for one of the Midlands National League teams based in Coventry. This franchise eventually came to Birmingham and became known as the Birmingham Bullets. The equivalent of this today would be getting scouted by a professional football club.

At school the PE teachers decided amongst themselves that I could only pursue only one sport and I was asked to choose between basketball and rugby. It wasn't really a tough decision for me because black kids don't like snow - I hated playing rugby in the snow and my response was *"I will stick with basketball because it's indoors."* Crazy I know, but neither sport was really a professional sport, and as such were subordinated to entertainment level because football was the only true English professional sport at the time. Obviously, the school tried to milk the story about one of their students representing the country. Subsequently, a small interview and photo shoot were arranged with a local paper that came to school and took some photos of me playing basketball. The three of us trained a few times for Team Fiat during the week and because of my commitments with them that year, I stopped going to church on Sundays as our matches were on a Sunday in Coventry. Ivor, Herman and I would meet at New Street station and go to Coventry together.

Each year Handsworth Park had a big bonfire and by now, attending this event had become a rite of passage for many young people. It was my last year at school and I was finally old enough to go out at night to the park. It was November 1978 and this was to be the last ever bonfire event held in that park, heralding the end of an era.

To clarify, by now I had been in the England team for a couple years and had attended numerous training weekends at Lilleshall, so I understood the process. One weekend, the England Basketball team were training at The Lilleshall National Sports Centre. Their plan was for the players to arrive on the Thursday night to attend orientation, sort out rooms/pairings and then chill for the evening. Naturally, it makes good sense for the organiser to have the participants attend the night before.

Orientation in those days was just what it said - an opportunity to meet up in the bar and get drunk. As with most groups, the team had already formed into cliques and I always roomed with the same two guys, Ivor and Herman, who always had my spot in the room on hold for me. It was not uncommon for certain players to join the training sessions later. However, they were accompanied by their 'shaker mover' parents who would buddy up with the coaches and give an excuse for their child's absence directly to them. I don't recall any black parents ever attending any sporting events with their children, who were almost always unaccompanied and at the mercy of teachers and sports coaches. It was stupid of me to think and, even worse, dare to suggest that I should be allowed to travel alone, of my own volition, to join the group at Lilleshall the next day.

On receiving the letter informing me of the date of the intended training, I realised it clashed with my plans. The notice period had been relatively short and I already had commitments that I could no longer get out of. I quickly informed my PE teacher that due to personal reasons, it would not be convenient for me to attend the orientation on the Thursday evening. Upon hearing this, his whole demeanour changed; his face reddened and he became very animated as he expressed his total shock at my statement. To my total dismay, he shouted *"If you don't go to Lilleshall on Thursday as planned, you won't be able to go at all"*. At this point, it became clear to me that he did not respect my openness. I could have faked a 'sicky' and in hindsight that may have been the best course of action. But here we were *at the crossroads'*.

My plans had been made some considerable time before being notified of the date of the England team training session and just as I would today, I followed my heart and stuck with my decision. So that evening I went with my original plan and attended the Bonfire; a decision that had serious repercussions.

Just like any normal Friday morning during term time, I arrived at school. However, instead of being allowed into registration I was sent straight to the headmaster's office. Inside the office were the lower school headmaster and the PE Teacher. The headmaster set out his case for suspension and summarily suspended me from school until my parents arrived to hear my case. I couldn't believe it - I wanted to smash the office up but held my emotions in check. Picking up my bag, I turned and left the office and went to the bus stop to await my bus home. I'd been at this school for five years and my brother a year ahead of me and in all that time I don't think they had ever asked if my parents knew what sports I participated in or asked anything at all about my parents. Oh, except the cash to pay expenses for me to play. What did they think my dad was going to say about me not going to training for sport? In certain sports like horse racing, cricket, wrestling, and maybe even boxing, my dad was definitely an expert but he didn't have a clue about basketball. Nothing had been done by me to warrant exclusion and I thought my dad would have been angry at them because it was not about school work or attendance.

Arriving home, at approximately 9.50am, I opened the front door walking in confidently and heard my dad shout out *"a who dat?"* I replied *"a me"* and started to climb the stairs up to his room where he was in bed trying to get some sleep after his night shift. I explained to him what had happened and he got up and dressed and we jumped in the car and returned to Great Barr School to see the headmaster.

The office door opened and my dad and I moved orwards towards the open office. However, the headmaster lifted his hand showing me his palm, indicating that I should stay put, and only my dad was invited into the office; leaving me standing outside. Expecting to hear shouting coming from the office I thought my dad would represent me; however I knew that it would be a case of a picture being painted about their own view to my dad. Of course I was the student and should have said *"yes sir"* to every instruction that had been given to me.

My dad came out of the office slowly, in a courteous manner, with his head bowed and his brown trilby in his hand spinning it by the brim before placing it on his head in the corridor. He walked towards me and I stood to my full height in anticipation of his anger at what they had done to me - his son. Instead my dad started to cuss me in patois and began swinging punches at me. I blocked his punches and pushed him away so that there was some distance between us. Feeling shocked, angry and vexed all at the same time, I grabbed my bag and walked off down the corridor, outside to the Dyas Road entrance gate and went to Paul's house where we chilled out for the rest of the day. That was the day the relationship with my dad changed forever.

Following this incident, I asked myself, when did participating in 'out of school' sports activities get someone suspended from school for not attending training? My parents sent me to school to get an education as per the curriculum, but somewhere along the way someone decided that my out of school activity carried more weight than my in school activity. Basically, the school stopped teaching me. The whole incident with the school escalated to proportions that made it impossible for me to forgive the teacher for his hostility towards me, and no one tells me what to do. He threatened me with suspension but forgive me, I don't respond well to threats; furthermore, what did he think I was, a puppet? There are no strings on me and I was not prepared to be manipulated. I knew right there, at that moment, that it was all over and in my opinion it was no longer about basketball training but a case of them bullying me.

Obviously, when I had informed them that it would not be possible for me to attend on the Thursday, as requested, the battle lines had already been drawn by the teacher. After leaving the office, my mind began spinning with thoughts about the teacher's response to me and how much time I had contributed to making his basketball team into a success. I was the only school boy out there with them and subsequently, the one who wasn't doing their homework at night. Instead, I was wasting my time travelling around the West Midlands with a bunch of old men indulging in their common passion. They knew that poor outcomes at school would leave me with little options in life. Following this incident the relationship between the teacher and me became completely and irreconcilably damaged.

I was always of good character, a great student and achieved good results from assessments through school testing and in exams. My results kept me in the top 20% of all students in my year and my attendance was 100% notwithstanding all the sporting accomplishments, which were exemplary.

I played for the school teams, the regional team, the national and international team, as well as a club team. In addition to this I was also playing national league with Team Fiat in Coventry. All this took time, which I reckon totalled more than sixty hours per week, including travel, practice and play. Basketball success reduced the time I had to study and took me away from books. I can honestly say there is not a single thing that basketball taught me that a book could not have taught me better. But my question then, as is now, how many players from the UK have managed to succeed in the NBA? The answer is none.

Did the school not know that I had to take exams that summer? Now, it is hard for me to see exactly how I managed to get through school exams with so much time away playing basketball. But there was no telling us at that age that this was not the best thing to be doing. It would have helped greatly if even only one coach had set their personal ambitions aside and enquired after my welfare or educational expectations and possibilities. There was so much hype surrounding basketball that even in school, some form teachers suggested that I miss a lesson to go and practice basketball in the gym.

I left Great Barr School armed with the knowledge that there was a place for me at Broadway School and not only would I be able to add to my qualifications, for the first time in five years I would be able to go freely to school without the nagging fear of being physical and verbally assaulted by white men on my way home each evening.

Sixth Form School Move

I had been engaging with students and staff at Broadway for a number of years so jumped at the option to attend the school to play basketball as well as experiencing a black school which was more of a reward than punishment. In my sixth form year in March came the basketball finals time. Broadway hosted a team like no other team probably before or since. Broadway was able to field ten England players in one team such was the dominance of the school. I had changed schools and joined the team and the music group. In an almost replay of the breakdown in the relationship between myself and PE staff at Great Barr School it was about to happen at Broadway, all over again.

One evening we arrived at the sports hall to play a game. To us it was just another game; we were always confident and if we lost, then so what! Looking into the sports hall, we soon determined that something was wrong. The score table had not been put out and the coach was not in the room. We went to the coach's office and saw that he was on the phone in deep discussion. As we drew closer, it became apparent that he was talking to the coach from the other school as they wanted to cancel the game on the day. The reason being was that their star player had an exam the next day and they felt it prudent for him to be revising the day before an exam. At first it didn't mean a thing but it soon became clear that the arrangements being made would have an effect on something we had already planned for the following week. I tried to catch the coach's attention by frantically waving my hands around in front of his face whilst he was still speaking on the phone. He saw me, but he just ignored my attempts to butt into his conversation to inform him about the potential problem. He concluded his discussion with the other coach and merely confirmed that he would be travelling down to the school next week with or without us.

Personally, I have always hated the term 'or else', and this was for sure another 'or else' moment. I explained that as a group we had raised and committed a great deal of money and paid for a recording studio which was booked for the following week - the same time that he had just agreed to have the basketball game. We, being Tracey, Ivor and myself, urged him to call back and rearrange the game based on the new information provided to him now. He just stared at us and flatly said no. This was a slap in the face to me. Why was he being so unreasonable?

Sporting Dilemma

We were the only school in the country, then and now, that had an entire team that comprised solely of England players. A big thing was made of our visits with banners welcoming the 'England All Stars.' The embarrassing thing for the coach was that his two main players were not present. The game would have been a formality if we had taken part but that was not to be the case and they were beaten comprehensively for the first time all season.

Whilst our school basketball team were getting whooped playing the match, all three of us got suspended for not attending. Meanwhile, the band were at Earth studio setting up for our very first recording session with 'Wholligan' and 'Waldo'.

Earth Studio – Perry Barr

We paid for four hours of studio time and it was simply a case of how many tracks we could record and mix in that time. Everything in the studio looked technical and complicated, from the mixer board with hundreds of knobs and dials everywhere through to the various reel to reel tape machines dotted around the room. We felt like we were on board a space ship or in the cockpit of an aeroplane. During the session Winston Douglas, our technician/engineer, was constantly shouting instructions to us through the partition glass which was between the recording booth and studio room and simultaneously having intensive discussions with 'Wholligan', the engineer and producer of the session. We hadn't musically prepared anything beforehand. It was just a case of making it up as we went along – in fact it was a case of someone saying *"unuh gwaan, just do a tune"*. We already had a number of dubs that rocked the house whenever we performed live, which seemed a good place to start. The lead vocalist ad libbed over the drum and bass tracks and put in a harmony line and 'Wholligan' would encouragingly say *"Yes I hear dat one deh, it sound like da bom"*.

As beginners, we trusted the engineers to know what was being played in the dance halls like Canterbury as at the time our music was dancehall music and not radio play music. By the end of the session we had recorded two tracks, 'Pope Paul' and 'Babylon Crash'. The music was definitely foundation music and 'Wholly' had a field day doing the mix, particularly for Pope Paul. At the end of the session everyone was immensely satisfied with the product and 'Wholligan' kept the recording of the 'Pope Paul' dub-plate for Orthodox Sound. These were our first recordings and the beginning of a commitment to music.

Déjà Vu

It was the morning after and the day of reckoning for the lynching. We were promptly brought before the great white Massa (Headmistress), to a disciplinary for non-attendance at an after school activity that we had informed staff we would not be attending one week beforehand.

It felt like a flashback to Great Barr School. The song '96 Degrees' by Third World says it all:

"They taking InI, to see a big fat boy,
sent from overseas, the Queen employ.
Excellency before you I stand with my
representation,
you know where I'm coming from.
You catch me on the loose fighting to be free,
now you show me a noose under cotton tree,
entertainment for you, martyrdom for me"

Throughout the proceedings, the coach urged the headmistress to suspend us from school because he wanted us punished and insisted on an apology from us as we had *'let the school down'*. This was laughable and I point-blank refused but distinctly remember Ivor apologising to the Massa like a good nigger. Ivor was undecided, he didn't want to let either the group or the basketball coach down but since he had spent his money to attend the studio session, like the rest of us, he was also obligated.

The headmistress told us that she had *"seen many young people pursue music careers"* but, *"it was a waste of time"* and that we would *"never have any success."* She then suspended us from school for a few days. I was VEX at the disproportional response - we had not actually done anything wrong - it was an outside of school hours matter. The anger in me was overwhelming and I cussed the coach and shouted all sorts of expletives.

"As I walked out the door toward the gate that would lead to my freedom, I knew if I didn't leave my bitterness and hatred behind, I'd still be in prison."
Nelson Mandela

PLAYLIST 2

EARLY ROOTS MUSIC

EARLY ROOTS MUSIC

The Versatiles - Cutting Razor
Lacksley Castell - Jah Love Is Sweeter
Pablo Moses - Give I Fe I Name
Bunny Wailer - Rise & Shine
Dennis Brown - Concentration
Earl Lowe - Jah Can Count On I
Horace Andy - Never Tell I
John Holt - Every Day Is Just A Holiday
Ranking Caretaker - No Dash It Wey
Abyssinians - Oh Lord
African Brothers - Mystery Of Nature
African Stone - Run Rasta Run
Al Barry & The Cimarons - Morning Sun
Al Campbell - Gone Down The Drain, Clean Hand,
Cruising , Down In A Babylon, Jah Army, Oversize
Man, Rasta Time, Take A Ride, Repatriation
Alric Forbs- Jah Knows It's True
Alton Ellis & Zoot - Oppression
Anthony Johnson - I Am Coming Home, Gunshot
Aswad - Back To Africa
Augustus Pablo - King Tubby Meets Rockers Uptown
Jacob Miller - Baby I Love You So
Bagga - Daughter Of Zion
Barrington Spence - Don't Tutch I Dread
Barry Brown - Fittest Of The Fittest, Catch Them

Jah Jah, No Wicked Shall Enter The Kingdom Of
Zion, Far East, Give Another Israel A Try, Big Big
Politician
Big Youth - House Of Dread Locks, I Love The Way
You Love
Big Youth - Keep Your Dread
Black Uhuru - Darkness, One Love, Abortion, Fit You
Haffe Fit
Folk Song, Shine Eye Gal, Sinsemilla, Sponji Reggae, I
Love King Selassie, Puff She Puff, What Is Life
Bob Marley & The Wailers - Coming In From
The Cold, Could You Be Loved, Crazy Baldhead,
Guiltiness, Is this Love, Rastaman Vibration, Satisfy
My Soul, Selassie Is The Chapel, Slave Driver, Sun Is
Shining, Cry To Me, Small Axe, Waiting In Vain, Turn
Your Lights Down Low
Bob Marley Ft Ras Michael - Rastaman Chant,
Gonna Get You, Stay With Me
Bunny Wailer - Rastaman, Riding, Fig Tree,
Armagideon
Blackstones - Open the Gates
Burning Spear - Down By The River, Foggy Road, Jah
No Dead, Christopher Columbus
Bobby Culture - Health & Strength
Bobby Melody - Got To Be Stern, Jah Bring I Joy (In
The Morning), Mutty Mutty Girl
Black Notes - Open The Gates
Creole - Beware
Creole - Jah Creation
The Congos - Lost Sheep
Cornell Campbell - Natty Dread In A Greenwich

Farm, Blessed Are They, Hear Mi Now Star, Help Them
Jah Jah
Carlton & The Shoes - Happy Land, What A Day
Carlton Livingston - Fret Them A Fret, Trodding
Through The Jungle
Carol Kalphat - African Land
Creation - Enter Into His Gates With Praise
Culture - Down In Jamaica, Stop The Fussing And
Fighting
Culture & Prince Mohammed - Zion Gate/Forty Leg
Dread
Dennis Brown - Africa, Bloody City, Changing Times,
Cheater
Created By The Father , Tenement Yard, The
Prophet Rides Again, Black Liberation, Their Own
Way, Things In Life, To The Foundation, We All Are
One, Weep And Moan, Wolves And Leopards, Rasta
Children, At The Foot Of The Mountain, Hooligan,
Love And Hate
Dennis Brown/Aswad - Promised Land
Dennis Brown & Barry Biggs - Work All Day
Delroy Washington - Give All The Praise To Jah
Delroy Wilson - Beat Down Babylon
Don Carlos - Conscious Rasta
Earth & Stone - Sweet Africa, Give Me , Wicked A Fe
Dress Back
Errol Holt - Congo Dread
Fred Locks - The Little House, Black Star Liner, Don't
Let Babylon Use You, I Saw Rastafari, I've Got A Joy,
Love And Only Love, Sons Of The Almighty, Time To
Change, True Rastaman, Walls, Sing-A-Long

Freddy Mckay - Rome
Gladiators - I'm A Rebel, Jah Works, Bongo Red
Gladstone Anderson - Rockers
Hugh Mundell - Great Tribulation, King Of Israel, Let's
All Unite, Run Revolution A Come, Africa Must Be
Free, Rasta Have The Handle, Red, Gold And Green,
Jah Fire Will Be Burning
Hugh Mundell As Jah Levi - Why Do Black Man Fuss
And Fight
Lacksley Castell - Black Sheep
Horace Andy - Government Land
Hue B - Give Thanks And Praise
Ijahman Levi - Africa, We A Warrior, Jah Heavy
Load, I Am A Levi
Ijahman And Madge - I Do
I Roy - Satta-Amasa-Gana
Israel Vibration - Why Worry
The Black Survivors - Every Knee Shall Bow
Jacob Miller - Chapter A Day, I'm Just A Dread, Who
Say Jah No Dread, Zion Gates, 80,000 Careless
Ethiopians
Jah Larry - King Majesty
The Jay Tees - Forward To Jah
Johnny Clarke - Give Up The Badness, Enter His
Gates, Move Out of Babylon, None Shall Escape The
Judgement, Play Fool Fe Get Wise, Poor Marcus,
Every Knee Shall Bow, Can't Leave Jah, Declaration
of Rights
Joseph Hill - Behold The Land
Judah Eskender Tafari - Rastafari Tell You
Judy Mowatt - Black Woman, Mellow Mood, Slave

Queen
Justin Hinds & The Dominoes - Tell Me Not of Other
Lands
 Justin Hinds - Let Jah Rise
Jah Lion - Soldier And Police War
Jah Stitch & Johnny Clarke - True Born African
Ken Boothe - Black, Gold And Green
Kiddus I - Fire Burn, Harder
King Medious - This World
King Tubby & The Aggrovators - A Rougher Version
King Tubby & Yabby You - Jah Mercies
Lloyd Parks - Mafia
Larry Marshall - Run Babylon
Larry Marshall & The Evernears - The Ark Of Jah
Covenant
Junior Byles - Beat Down Babylon
Lee Perry - Roast Fish And Corn Bread
Linval Thompson - I Love Marijuana, Don't Cut Off
Your Dreadlocks, Jah Jah The Conqueror, Jamaican
Colley (Version), King Tubby Style, Marijuana Tree,
Never Conquer
Lion Youth - Rat A Cut Bottle
Little John & Toyan - Jah Guide I
Little John - Smoke Ganja Hard
Little Roy - Prophecy, Touch Not My Locks,
Christopher Columbus
Lizard - Satta I
Lloyd Jones - Daydreaming Of Africa
Marcus Reid - Poor Man Cry
Marcus Reid & The Dedicators - Why
Max Romeo - Chase The Devil, Melt Away, One Step

Forward, Valley Of Jehosaphat, War Ina Babylon
Michael (Cane Juice) Marsh - Ghetto Tenement Yard
Michael Rose - Guess Who's Coming To Dinner
Errol Dunkley - Movie Star
Mighty Diamonds - Long Time, Every Other Day,
I Need A Roof, Shame And Pride, Conversation,
Country Living, Have Mercy, Natural Natty, Right
Time, Back Weh, Pass The Kutchie
Mighty Fantels - Everywhere
Mighty Threes - Rasta Business
Mighty Soul Rebels - Jah Jah Is No Gimmick
Niney - Blood And Fire
Naggo Morris - Su Su Pon Rasta
Nathan Skyers - Matter Of Time
Omar Bernard - Man A Kill Man
Owen Gray - Rizla
Palmer Brothers - Step It Out A Babylon
Patrick Andy - Every Tongue Shall Tell
Paul Blackman - Earth Wind & Fire
Peter Tosh - Legalise It, Stepping Razor
Phil Pratt All Stars - What About The Half
Instrumental
Philip Fraser - Come Ethiopians, Have Faith In
Rastafari,
Mr Wicked Man
Prince Far I - Deck Of Cards
Ranking Dread - Africa
Ras Ibuna - Diverse Doctrine
Ray I - Kunta Kinte Black Roots
Reggae Regular - Where Is Jah
Rock Tone Band - Promised Land

Rocky Music - Struggle
Rod Taylor - Ethiopian Kings, His Imperial Majesty
Roman Stewart - No Peace Until, Praise Jah
Ronnie Davis - Every Rasta Is A Star
Ruddy Thomas/Trinity - Everyday Is Just A Holiday/
Natty Dread On The Go
Rudolph Francis & Ranking Blake - Mr Oppressor
The Silvertones - Make A Joyful Noise
Aisha - Guide And Protect
Rasheda/Mystickal - I Love Jah/Jah Love
The Viceroys - Heart Made Of Stone
Sly & Robbie - Dread Rastafari, We Are Africa
Sonny Washington - Black Skin
Sons of Jah - Tubby's Vengeance
Steel Pulse - Klu Klux Klan
Steel Pulse - Handsworth Revolution
Sugar Minott - King Of Kings, Strictly Sensi
Sylford Walker - Burn Babylon, Chant Down Babylon,
Jah Golden Pen
I & I - Armageddon Rock
Tapper Zukie - Man from Bosrah, Don't Get Crazy
Tapper Zukie Featuring Bob Marley - Give Thanks
Tetrack - Only Jah Know
The Abyssinians - Love Comes And Goes, Abendigo,
Satta Massagana, Sweet Feeling, This Land Is For
Everyone
The Chosen Brothers - March Down Babylon
The Congos - Fisherman
The Ethiopians - Hail Rasta, Brother Hail
The Gladiators - A Prayer To Thee, Cant Stop
Righteousness, Declaration Of Rights, Eli Eli, Hearsay,

Jah Works, Looks Is Deceiving, Roots Natty Roots,
That Nuh Right, The Rich Man Poor Man, Pretending
The Heptones - Mama Say
The Itals - Give Me Power, In A Dis Ya Time,
Satisfaction
The Light of Saba - Words Of Wisdom
The Marijuanas - Tell Us When
The Mighty Diamonds - Go Seek Your Rights, Jah Will
Work It Out, Know Your Culture, Stand Up To Your
Judgement, Them Never Love Poor Marcus
The Mighty Diamonds & Ranking Joe - Just Like A
River
The Mighty Maytones - Praise Jah, Who Can't Hear
Must Feel
The Morwells - Be Wise
The Prophets - Warn The Nation
Jah Stitch & The Prophets - Judgement Style
The Twinkle Brothers - Jahoviah, Never Get Burn,
Since I Throw The Comb Away
The Wailing Souls - Jah Jah Give Us Life To Live
Soul Syndicate Featuring Tony Tuff - Chant Down
Babylon
Tony Tuff - Run Come Come
The Twinkle Brothers - Chant Down Babylon, Keep
On Trying, Rasta Pon Top
U Roy - Joyful Locks
Valentine Brodie - Life In The Ghetto
Velvet Shadows - Babylon A Fall Down
Wailing Souls - Fire House Rock, A Day Will Come, A
Fool Will Fall, Act of Affection, All Alone, Baby Come
Back, Bredda Gravalicious, Inchpinchers, Jah Jah

Give Us life, Kingdom Rise kingdom Fall, Old Broom, Very Well
Wayne Chin & Creole - Jah Creation
Wayne Jarrett - Brimstone & Fire, Every Tongue Shall Tell, Live And Love, You And I, Satta Dread
Wayne Smith - Ain't No Me Without You, Ism & Skism, Time Is A Moment In Space
Willie Williams - Armageddon Time
Winston Francis - Going To Zion, Lets Go To Zion
Winston Jarrett & The Righteous Flames - No Man's Land
Burning Spear - Jordan River
Yabby You - Deliver Me From My Enemies, Walls Of Jerusalem, Humanity Dub
Yabby You & The Prophets - Jah Love, Judgement Time
Yabby You & Michael Prophet - Mash Down Rome
Yabby You & Wayne Wade Mr. Eastwood - Ballistic Dread
Yabby You & Trinity - Chant Down Babylon Kingdom
Yami Bolo - Jah Made Them All

3

I HAVE A DREAM

Black Wax Record Shop

People from Aston encountered suffering in their everyday lives and as a result a fertile environment grew which fostered musical successes and businesses. The experience of suffering empowers people to develop the musicality skills within them, whether it be writing, producing or setting up their own music trade.

Along with the already established sound systems, there was a demand from the large enthusiastic Caribbean community to own records from home (Jamaica). It provided a 'vibe' that was designed to evoke an emotional response, a memory that grasped the heart strings of listeners. Music provided inspiration expressed through evolving the rhythms of Blue Beat, Ska, Rock Steady and eventually Reggae music.

Black Wax Record shop brought music to the streets of Aston and Handsworth. The pulsating vibrations of musical ecstasy saturated the minds of people and it was a place that 'spiritually rocked.' People travelled from afar to wallow in the experience of listening to the 'get together' music, which is what reggae music is. The shop was always busy and the shop assistant could be heard shouting *"who again?*

Come up front." meaning who else wants to buy. Completing transactions were usually followed by long, drawn out goodbyes like *"Irie-I, nice Jah man, respect brethren."* There is no such thing as a short 'goodbye' in Rasta lyrics.

Canterbury Cross

It's July 1975 and the beginning of the six week summer holidays; this had to be one of the most boring outlooks for me as a thirteen year old, because there were very few organised activities going on that year. Canterbury Cross was one of three Broadway School campuses, was situated on Whitehead Road, Aston and the other was the main Broadway site.

One day, my brother and I decided to go along to Canterbury youth club which had all-day pool and table tennis. As is the case with most pool tables, people would indicate their desire to play and mark their place. But there was a dark skinned 'screw face guy'; a very gruff figure dressed slightly differently from the rest of the youths with lots of chains and rings - he had what people now call 'swagger'. This guy, having just arrived at the pool table, decided to grab hold of the pool cue and declared that he was playing next, as though no one could say or do anything about it. I took matters into my own hands, walked around the pool table and grabbed hold of the pool cue. It was still firmly in his grasp and I started to get annoyed with the guy but it was clear that neither one of us was going to back down. Eventually, he let go of the cue and walked away 'running his mouth off.' I didn't know then that our paths would cross again in the near future.

The school holidays were over but there was a buzz on the streets - everyone was talking about the dances at Canterbury Cross School which were held in the basement of the old school annex every Monday, Wednesday and occasionally on Friday. Most of the youths who attended were predominantly from Aston and Handsworth, but youths travelled from all over the city to attend, as Canterbury was the place where Sound Systems made their reputations. Youths of all ages sneaked out of their bedroom windows and parents would often show up, invade the dance and beat their kids in public.

We grew up on reggae music and artists like Bob Marley brought what we needed - more conscious lyrics and positive messages. The lyrics provided information on topics that had not been discussed by our parents. This is reflected in the 'Canterbury Music' appendix as it was music that first told us that black people were not Caribbean, but African prisoners of war, taken into captivity in Africa and locked up in the Caribbean. Jamaican reggae music preached to people in a similar way that the churches' gospel music is used to signpost people back to God's message. Canterbury quickly became the heart and soul of the community and almost a rite of passage for our generation.

Many youths attended not only because they enjoyed it but because it helped them to escape the harsh racist world. They learnt more about the emerging black culture through music and vibes, enabling them to have a heightened knowledge of their roots through the music. The ability to release tension and be themselves with their peers gave them a freedom of expression that they had never experienced. Everybody became clothing conscious because they had to look 'stush' for Canterbury. Young 'Bubbo' dreads came in abundance and at the time 'dread girls' wore wraps, pleated skirts and moccasin shoes. The boys wore Clarks booties, beaver hats and had ratchet knives. Tailor cut trousers became the rage and I purchased my first pair from a tailor called Rough Cut on Westminster Road and as his name suggests, the trousers he made were always roughly cut. Older guys with cars and long dreads also came to rave alongside the youths. It was a happy hunting ground and teen pregnancy soared. It became the place where the 'good girls go bad', and it was packed every evening. There was public humiliation and scandal in church every Sunday, as younger sisters and brothers started skipping church service and going to Canterbury; many of the girls became pregnant and were shamed out of the church. This led to an increase in homelessness as youths got kicked out of their homes because they disobeyed their parents. Imagine getting home at 10.30pm and the door being locked by your parents. Seems crazy now but it was normal in the 70s.

With the emergence of the dances held at Canterbury, Broadway youths began to build their own sound systems to play against each other and against bigger sounds from Birmingham. Many students from Broadway and Holte Schools built sound systems by means fair and foul. Some of the greats are Nyah Esquire, Orthodox, Siffa, Black Heart, High Priest, Eternal Youth, Observer, and Bizmark sound systems.

One of the biggest sound systems that came out of Broadway was Jungle-man, which was the jewel in the crown, our champion. This crew was absolutely massive and unique. They secured funding and bought a massive PA system, consistent with rave tech used these days. They were real social entrepreneurs. They created a business that influenced a generation by making and retailing clothing, paraphernalia, hats and bags, which they marketed all over the world. They had a brand and a worldwide presence. Many of the local crews, whether groups or sound systems, were comprised of a rich mix of boys from different schools, families, or simply living in the same area.

Parents became increasingly frustrated with their children deciding to follow the Jamaican Rastafarian faith culture. When parents forbade their children from playing in their homes what they called Rasta music, the response would be *"You nuh hear me tell you nuh fe listen to dat damn foolishness in yah?"* For those who dared to commit the crime of growing locks, they were soon confronted with *"Come out, come out. You can't stop in yah wid dat deh dutty head enuh, you fava damn thief, come outta me yard."* Thus, the decision to become Rastafarians meant that they had to leave home whilst others left simply because they wanted to.

Black parents are famous for stating the obvious like *"this is my house"* normally whilst stamping feet and throwing what looks somewhat like a childish tantrum. My parents' favourite line was "this is my house" and then insisting that you obey them in their house or leave. In reality this statement was effectively the death sentence for many a relationship and the absolute beginning of the demise of the very idea of a black community. For many, those lonely nights away from the family home in unpopular social housing flats led to the phenomena known as the 'baby mother' and 'baby father'. As a black boy in the street at that time it seemed as if the whole world was changing around me.

Broadway Music Scene

There was a reggae band in every school year and the school had a rich tradition of the bands that had gone on before. Bands like Eclipse, Delegation and JALN. Broadway was so much more vibrant than Great Barr, the environment felt welcoming like a community hub, maybe as a result of rich sports, music, and the fittest girls. On any given day of any week of the year, 'Nuff' of the black youths from the other schools would congregate at Broadway after school just to 'chill out' in what became a safe haven for people like me.

The school was full of personalities like Amlak (Steel Pulse) and his crew who were in the year below us. I eventually learned that Amlak went to Holte Comprehensive, another black school on the ends, but because his family and mates were at Broadway he was always around after school. So like me he was adopted into legend and folk law. There were also Myki Tuffis and the Salam Foundation crew who were in the year below Amlak.

Alongside the bands were many individual artists, some of whom were amazing singers - like Lyte Powell, Rob-I Ranks, Eddy, Rose Capri and a world of DJs and talented MCs. A few guys who were 'sound system' engineers threw their lot in with Mr Waldo and opened a recording studio around the corner from the school. Waldo did the business end and the others were given license to fly and become great producers of the time. One of them was the producer Whooligan, our own equivalent of Mad Professor, who produced the first single by Apache Indian. Another mega engineer/producer from school was Father Spears, who was renowned for producing Pato Banton's music. The two guys are still working today and may have the 'Holy Grail', master tapes from a generation of Birmingham's artists. Winston Douglas was another sound engineer and did all the Unity-related work.

The idea of joining a band was implanted at the back of my mind whilst at Great Barr School. Some of the older lads, Dave Parry and Chris, started a music group which rehearsed in the middle school hall after school each day and I was one of the first to join them at practice. Musicians were few and far between and the main candidates - in fact, the only candidates - were 'Blackeye', Clive, Ian and 'Tassi'. They brought guitars and an amplifier with them, because the only instruments available to use were an old drum kit and school piano. Both of the guitars were plugged into the amplifier and I recall playing one song with them, a song which was popular at the time called Easy, by Lionel Ritchie and the Commodores. However, compared to Broadway, Great Barr was uninspiring, lifeless, drab and characterless and there was a lack of opportunity to meet likeminded peers.

By contrast, Broadway was vibrant, the atmosphere was exhilarating and there was the opportunity to meet new people with a common interest; however, the greatest thing was that my peers were like me – black!

Unity Group Invitation

Ivor and I had become firm friends mainly because of the sheer volume of time we spent together playing basketball. One day the conversation turned to music. After telling him that I played the guitar at church, he spoke about the band that was at his school and invited me to attend a rehearsal. To my surprise, a lot of the members were already known to me. The founder of the band was Lloyd, the main vocalist. He had three female vocalists; Dawn, Margaret, and Michelle. Their performances on stage made them the envy of every girl in the school and the desire of every man. It was a hard time for the girls as they were actively being sought by the 'hungry belly boys' of the time. The girls were definitely hot property and they knew it. The popularity of each of the girls was apparent and as the new kid on the block, I observed them with a certain amount of fascination amidst the throngs of their male admirers. They were each solo artists within their own right.

I was shocked seeing Francis, the very same guy that I was going to batter at Canterbury when he clashed with my brother the previous summer. Francis was not only a talented drummer but also a great songwriter. The band wrote really good songs that were about real issues, songs that people could sing along to. I can honestly say that on the strength of Francis's song writing and the talent of vocalist Lloyd, I joined the Unity band.

One of the band's first tracks was written by Francis and was called It's a Hard Life Living in Aston:

"The way that Aston is situated, it so hard and complicated, the efforts of black people do not seem to be appreciated. Got to work so hard every day,

just to get your-self a little pay, Got to pay for my
food got to pay my rent, at the end of the day ain't
got nothing left. It's a hard life."

I was extremely impressed with this song and
another called 'Unity':

"Every day we look at society, there ain't no
change, no diplomacy, in India, there is poverty and
in Africa problems with equality."

On keyboards was Plug, with Anthony on bass.
Anthony's dad also played bass in a band called The
Black Diamonds. There were two guitarists, Tracey
and Andrew, who I already knew from junior
school, and finally Ivor on percussion. Of course
there was also Winston, who was the unshakable
sound engineer of the day.

Francis and I became friendly and we went on to
become great friends. I spent many evenings with
him 'chillaxing' and reasoning at his mother's
house on Wilton Road. He was very cultured
compared to other religious people I knew and
was one of the first people to speak seriously about
what we call 'consciousness'. A massive old Bible,
which was always left open on the verse that he
would read that day, would be the first thing that
you would see upon entering his house. Francis
spoke of His Majesty with authority and with
clarity that others struggled to achieve. He stressed
the importance of knowing one's self and culture

which he said is Rastafari consciousness and spoke about Rastafari's tenets, origins and rituals. He based his whole appearance on the principles of His Majesty explaining the power of the stones which he wore and the physical and spiritual connection. Francis also explained that His Majesty said *"It's not a black and white thing. His Majesty tells us not to watch colour and things like that. We just look at the integrity and behaviour of a man"*.

Following the wealth of information received from Francis and the fact that this information was not taught in school, I conducted my own research to further my knowledge.

Broadway Rehearsals

The group rehearsed after school each day in the music room at Broadway. The room was basically a breeze block reverb chamber with a few instruments placed in it for good measure. The equipment was dire and limited to a few pieces of drum kit, one amplifier that everyone plugged into, including the singers.

Soon after my first visit to rehearsal, I was whisked off to a house in Townley Gardens to meet Paul, the manager of the group. The meeting took place at the Bassaragh family home. There were a couple of guys in the living room, Paul and Eton, Paul's younger brother. Eton had the most spectacular Afro and was a great footballer. He was also a legendary dancer at Canterbury, incredibly witty and full of jokes. We stayed there for some time talking and everyone seemed totally relaxed and at ease. Paul, a Jamaican with a passion for music, was always full of bravado.

We weren't aware that anyone else was in the house when suddenly the living room door burst open. There stood a vision, a most incredibly beautiful Jamaican Indian girl. Sharon, Paul and Eton's younger sister, was scantily clad; dressed in a silk night dress covered by a silk night gown. She was 'cocky confident' and strolled into the room holding her dressing gown closed. Suddenly, the whole room faded to black around me and my mouth dropped open uncontrollably. A few seconds later I caught myself staring too hard at her but I tried to style it out pretending that I was not looking. As she bent down to get a cigarette from the pack on the table, she lifted it to her mouth, my eyes followed her every movement. She asked for a light, at which point Eton passed a lighter to her. She stood up with the lighter to the cigarette inhaling and then exhaled the smoke entirely through her thick lips into the air. Paul shouted through the hatch, *"Sharon, this is Hulk"*. All of a sudden she turned her head, looked towards me and said, *"Oh! Hello!"* Busy wiping the saliva from my lips, I extended my hand towards her in order to greet her. Sharon blew cigarette smoke in my face before asking *"So are you joining the group then?"* I responded, *"Yeah, yes"*, stumbling over my words. I started to banter with her for a while and suddenly heard the sound of heavy footsteps speedily coming down the stairs. To my surprise it was 'Saddo' Barber, from Great Barr School. 'Saddo' was surprised to see me and shouted out *"HULK!"* whilst bending down to get a cigarette from the pack that was on the table. He 'kotched' the cigarette in his lips and began telling everyone about school whilst searching under piles of coats and bags on the settee for his clothing. 'Saddo' was already a lower case 'god' but now he got elevated to an upper case 'God' status in my mind.

Paul, Eton and Sharon's dad was called Beelow. Beelow was a very short stocky Jamaican Indian man, an infamous character, particularly amongst our posse as we congregated at his house on a daily basis. It would be fair to say that alcohol was acceptable and widely used amongst the family members. They all knew what their dad's general movements were and roughly what time he would return home which would normally be the cue to leave through the opposite door. One night, a large group of us were at their house messing about. People were always looking to test me, and one 'not so clever man' decided that they would all rush me and hold me down. I screamed out crammmmmp! Unfortunately, Cleveland was holding the leg in which I had the cramp. He was squarely on the end of my foot as I reacted by extending my leg to its maximum length. I looked up and saw Cleveland flying backwards through the air, landing squarely inside Beelow's glass cabinet. The whole room went silent, even Cleveland, who at this point, was sitting in the cabinet on all the glass. Suddenly everyone burst into laughter. People were rolling around the floor holding their stomach from laughter. Cleveland, whilst still in shock, raised himself up from the broken glass which was all over him and then he too burst into laughter, setting everyone off again.

L.S.D Finch Road

I will never forget this gig as this was when the band's line up first changed. Francis, by nature, demanded more attention than any other members of the band and ensured that he had a say in all aspects of the music. Paul informed us that a booking had been made at the LSD club which was situated on the corner of Lozells Road. It was at that point that Francis declared, in his usual autocratic way, that he wasn't going to play at the gig.

Being young and having big egos, we were keen to perform and decided that we would perform without Francis if necessary. He was not pleased and got up from behind the drum kit and left rehearsal. This didn't pose too much of a problem as a few of the band members thought that they could play a one drop beat on the drum kit. Andrew was by far the best drummer amongst us, so the decision was made and we began to rehearse the songs without Francis; this did not affect the vocals, bass or rhythm sections.

We went to LSD straight after school and

were excited at the prospect of doing a gig. The performance area was a dark narrow room with tables strewn between the door and the dance floor with a large glass disco ball hanging from the ceiling. We began to set up the stage area and the drum kit and it wasn't long before the music balanced. The microphones were set up and the singers arrived to do a sound check with Lloyd. We had just finished the sound check when Francis arrived and we thought he had changed his mind about playing at the gig - we were wrong! Francis dismantled the drum kit, took the snare drum from the stand and put it under his arm and walked out of the club with it. Paul immediately jumped up and ran after Francis who told him that as he was not going to play he had come to get the drums, which he claimed were his, and leave the band behind for good. Paul went crazy and they both began to struggle with the snare drum. Francis eventually conceded before it got really serious. Francis was making a statement - if he wasn't there, then the band would not be performing. This was the last time we ever saw Francis in connection with the band.

The Cedar Club

The Cedar Club, situated in Hockley, was owned by one of the Fewtrell brothers. This was the most prestigious gig that we had managed to get to date. We were exuberant, keen and just like LSD, we went to the club straight from school. We entered through the entrance at the back and when we arrived, the bands were already setting up. Our turn came to sound check but the sound engineers had little or no interest in how our equipment actually sounded and only sought to ensure that the sound was coming through the mixing board.

On that particular day, the legend Doc Holiday, a notorious gangster, was in the house. We were still at school and this man was an elder of our little Jamaican community at the time. The Yardies arrived on stage and within a few minutes there was a completely different sound coming out of the PA system. This was the first time we graced the stage with one of our early idols, someone who had made a record and was also movie star. In real life, Horse Mouth Wallace was just like the character he played in the film *Rockers* and he dominated the proceedings. This left a lasting memory.

Trinity Road Rehearsals

Unity needed to find a new rehearsal room but we didn't know much about renting space or where we would be able to make a racket without anyone complaining too much.

One day Paul, the manager, announced that we were going to rent the cellar at Poncho's house for rehearsal. Poncho, Abbu's dad, agreed to make the cellar available to us at a weekly cost. As young entrepreneurs, we went to look at the cellar which was spacious enough but the height from floor to ceiling was only about 5' 5" in height. I stand at 6'5" so it meant that I would have to bend at all times in the room and would only ever be comfortable if I was sitting down whilst rehearsing. Poncho's house was a traditional house with a coal cellar but the stairway to the cellar was spacious enough to allow us to get equipment up and down without too much hassle. It was clean throughout and looked as though coal had never passed down those stairs.

The only problem was the height of the ceiling which didn't affect the vertically challenged amongst us, but we decided we would excavate the floor down another two feet and then start using it for rehearsal. Paul discussed the proposal with Poncho who expressed some concerns about hitting the gas main. Subsequently, Poncho started collecting rent off us - in advance. We began removing the brick flooring with the minimum damage so that we could re-use them once we had lowered the floor. We then dug out the cellar floor, and lowered it by approximately two feet. The coal hatch which led directly into the cellar was used to remove the rubble and to bring in the cement to seal the floor. We didn't use a spirit level or any other kind of measuring tool to determine the exactness of the work; only our judgement. After getting it flat and level, we replaced the bricks on top of the cemented floor. Amazingly, we did not hit any gas or water pipes and the whole operation went well and served as a massive motivational session. We redecorated and had power sockets fitted at various points in the room. Finally, after a couple of weeks, the cellar was ready and we moved in. At last, we had somewhere to setup our equipment and leave it at the end of rehearsals. This became the Unity HQ and we spent many nights in that rehearsal room compiling new tracks or chilling.

The Downside

We had been renting the cellar for a couple of months before strange things started to happen in the rehearsal room. Equipment was being used and moved around when we were not rehearsing. Poncho and his band rehearsed in the rear dining room of the house and it soon became apparent that they saw the availability of our rehearsal space as something that was beneficial to them. Firstly, he had easy access to our equipment and secondly, he could evict us and use the newly refurbished cellar as his own band's own rehearsal room rather than the rear dining room. In the end things just got farcical - we put our pocket money together to pay rent on time every week. However, in return Poncho and his band did not respect our efforts and ultimately disrespected us by using our equipment whenever they wanted. Once we discovered what had been going on, we objected which resulted in our immediate eviction from the cellar.

On a positive note, the experience had been a great team-building exercise and the venture gave us the opportunity to find out more about each other outside of the music sphere.

We got the work done, and we kept it together - even through the adversity.

The Vocalists

The girl vocalists were an integral part of the group, similar to the I Threes, the backing vocalists for Bob Marley. More often than not, one of them would turn up late to rehearsal. The problem was that as soon as the 'late girl' arrived, all three would stop rehearsing and share their personal problems, stories about guys that they were seeing or possibly just the 'passa-passa' that they relished. Lloyd would run a series of classic one-liners on them about their various issues. However, the time came when Lloyd no longer thought the situation was funny and began to cuss them for wasting rehearsal time. As far as he was concerned, they were not focused on getting their vocals right. Maybe, it became too difficult for them to juggle being in the group and dating. Eventually we said goodbye to each of the ladies for good. Now, Unity was five members lighter than when I had joined, having lost Francis, the ladies and Plug on keyboards.

It was decided that Andrew would become the permanent drummer and I took on the role of playing keyboards. We also recruited another guitarist to accompany Tracey. The band members were aware of Danny's guitar abilities and furthermore, he had his own equipment and would be able to commence rehearsing straight away. I approached Danny and asked him if he would be interested in joining the band and he agreed. Subsequently, the permanent re-birth of the new Unity group lineup became established as follows:

Unity Group Lineup

Vocalist	Lloyd
Drums	Andrew
Percussion	Ivor
Bass	Anthony aka Abbu
Guitar 1	Tracey
Guitar 2	Danny
Keyboards	Owen aka (Hulk)

Ghetto Gigs Scene

There were lots of pubs offering live entertainment and so gigs were relatively easy to come by for weekend warriors. There were loads of reggae bands from all over the city. Bands like Cornerstone, Beshara, Black Symbol, Senator and African Star would all play at different venues on the same night.

It was easy to get regular paid session work gigging with bands just for one night performances. The infamous Saxa from The Beat was one success story from the pub circuit of the day and as we know, he went onto achieve fame on the Two Tone scene.

The early days of Unity attracted a loyal and large

following of mainly school youths. As the band's music progressed, we ventured further afield and were able to secure regular gigs, up and down the country and many of our fans liked to tag along. I was also the van driver for the band, so my gig days tended to start with meeting Paul and then hiring a van. Whilst on the road, most of the band spent their time eating, smoking, sleeping or in discussion about the exploits of Tracey's Uncle Sydney or Eclipse, the group that Pato, Tracey's brother was a member of. My gig day tended to end at least an hour later than the rest of the band due to me having to return the vehicle.

We did a number of gigs over the coming years that provided us with invaluable experience about the business and stage craft. Some of the shows were at clubs in other cities in the UK.

The band organised several gigs at the West Indian club in Gloucester. Seven coaches were booked each time there was a gig and tickets sold out instantly. All the coaches were always full of enthusiastic fans – men, lots of women, music, food, weed and alcohol, all of which produced a nice vibe. Even the coach drivers got 'mash-up' and didn't mind us blazing as long as they could get into the clubs to rave the night away.

Central to the whole rave was the dance challenge. Some of the Gloucester crew used to 'Dally'. A dance was performed by both men and women and was known for its unique emphasis on intense shoulder movements, rolling the shoulder blades, bouncing the shoulders and jolting the chest. The Gloucester crew would bring challenger after challenger to test our posse. However, we had the world champion 'Dally' supreme in our camp. Eton was the Canterbury dallying champion and famous nationally for his amazing dance skills; he had moves which destroyed the crowd and totally embarrassed any challenger.

We loved the offstage entertainment as much as the performance. Having Eton around always made things get started in one way or another, and it often made our early gigs a much more memorable occasion.

We also did gigs at Huddersfield's Venn Street Club where every gig would be sold out. It was always a big thing when the Unity band was in town. It was almost our second home as we performed there both as a reggae and rock band. The after-party was always out on the Huddersfield blues scene, which was wicked. Lloyd's brothers were 'Kings' in Huddersfield as they had the champion sound system in Yorkshire. We always stayed at blues parties until morning light before moving on to the next stop.

We played at a gig with BB King at a festival in Toxteth. The venue was slap bang in the middle of a 'bomb peck'. The view outside the coach window was shocking - it seemed almost like a post-apocalyptic scene from a movie. None of us wanted to come off the coach to play on an old 'bomb peck' but once we got into the club and the music started blasting it turned out to be a good gig.

A night club in Birmingham called Locarno did not traditionally cater for black people. However, Monday nights became 'Soul' and 'Funk' night thus becoming a popular place for bands to perform. For us the gig at Locarno will always be one of the most memorable, as it's the place where Unity first earned the title Birmingham's best upcoming band. There was a rival band from Holte School, called Senator, who were our nemesis. Both bands yearned to be acclaimed as Aston's finest band so we were keen to make an impression at Locarno in front of the Birmingham fans. The battle was a big thing for us and on the day of the gig, we arrived early to do the sound check. All of us felt nervous about the show, but we really 'smashed' it. We had successive encores and became Birmingham's undisputed No 1 band and rulers of the Locarno era.

At this point in our journey, the music we listened to and were most influenced by, were exclusively artists from the 1975 era.

PLAYLIST 3

JAMAICAN LOVERS & RARE GROOVES

JAMAICAN LOVERS

Al Campbell - Gee Baby
Althea & Donna - Up Town Top Ranking
Alton Ellis - Let Him Try, Born Loser aka Black Man's Word, Breaking Up Is Hard To Do, Gonna Take A Miracle, I'm Still In Love With You Girl, Mr Ska Beena, Sitting In The Park, Too Late To Turn Back Now, You Make Me So Very Happy
Alton Ellis & U Roy - Ain't That Loving You
Barbara Jones - Changing Partners
Barry Brown - Rain From The Skies
Black Harmony - Don't Let It Go To Your Head
Blackstones - Girl Of My Dreams
Bob Andy - I've Got To Go Back Home, My Time
Bobby James - Let Me Go Girl
Bunny Maloney - Baby I've Been Missing You
Carl Malcolm - No Jestering
Carlton & The Shoes - Sweet Feeling, Love Me Forever
Cornell Campbell - Undying Love, Stars, My Confession, Conversation, Girl Of My Dreams, My One And Only Lover
Danny Ray - Play Boy
Delroy Wilson - Ain't That Loving You, Breaking Up, Sharing The Night Together, I Am Not A King, I'm Still Waiting, I've Been In Love, Moving Away, (It Looks Like) I'll Never Gonna Fall In Love Again, No More Heartaches,

146

Rain From The Skies, That's The Way Nature Planned It, Let Me Down Easy, This Love Of Mine

Derrick Harriott - The Loser

Dobby Dobson - Endlessly, This Is My Story

Ernest Wilson - Promise Me

Errol Dunkley - Give (If You Can Give), Happiness Forgets, O.K. Fred

Freddie Mckay - Picture On The Wall, When You're Smiling, Show And Tell

Ginger Williams - I Can't Resist Your Tenderness, In My Heart There's A Place

Gregory Isaacs - Let's Dance

Honey Boy - Impossible Love

Hortense Ellis - Unexpected Places

In Crowd - Baby My Love

Inner Circle – Groovin' In Love

Jayes & Ranking Trevor - Born To Love/All I Have Is Love

Jimmy London - Till I Kiss You

John Holt - Again, Doctor Love, I'll Be Lonely, It May Sound Silly, Never Let Me Go, Stick By Me, Stranger In Love, Touch Me In The Morning, Walk Away, You'll Never Find Another Love Like This, A love I Can Feel

Johnny Clarke - Everyday Wondering, Please Don't Go, My Desire

Junior English - Ready To Learn

Ken Boothe - Its Gonna Take A Miracle, That's The Way Nature Planned It, Walk Away From Love

Ken Parker - Jimmy Brown

Larry Marshall - I Admire You

Leroy Simmons - At The Dance

Linval Cooper - Happy Birthday
Lloyd Charmers - For The Good Times, Sweet Harmony
Lloyd Parks & Big Youth - No War In The Dance
Lord Creator - Kingston Town
Marcia Aitkin - I'm Still In Love
Marcia Griffiths - Mark My Word, Truly
Milton Henry - Gypsy Woman
Natural Touch - Gimme Good Loving
Nicky Thomas - Have A Little Faith
Pat Kelly - Queen Of The Minstrel
Pat Kelly & Dillinger - Talk About Love/First The Girl
The Techniques - Queen Majesty
Fil Calender & Jah Stitch - Baby My Love
Phyllis Dillon - Picture On The Wall
Prince Alla - Bucket Bottom
Richard Ace - Can't Get Enough
Slim Smith - The Time Has Come, Turning Point
Slim Smith & The Uniques - My Conversation
Otis Gayle - I'll Be Around
Tamlins - Baby Love
The Cables & Dennis Alcapone - Baby Why/Version
The Chantells - Waiting In The Park
Chosen Few - Love Between A Boy And Girl
The Heptones – Fatty Fatty aka I Need a Fat Girl, Pretty Looks, I Hold the Handle, I'm In The Mood For Love
The Invaders - Sweet Soul Rocking
The Sensations - Baby Love
Tamlins - Ting A Ling
The Techniques - I'm In The Mood, My Girl, Queen

Majesty
Tyrone Taylor - Cottage In Negril
Winston Groovy - Please Don't Make Me Cry

RARE GROOVES

7 Miles High - She's Gone Away
Adriana Evans - Looking For Your Love, Never Thought
Al Jarreau - We're In This Love Together
Jean Carne Featuring Al Johnson - I'm Back For More
Alicia Myers - I Want To Thank You
Angela Johnson featuring Darien - All In Me
Anglo Saxon Brown - Call On Me
Anita Baker - Feel The Need
Aretha Franklin - Rock Steady
Arnold Blair - Trying To Get Next To You
Art Webb - You Can't Hide Love
Ashford & Simpson - Bourgie Bourgie, Love Or Physical
Atlantic Star - Touch A Four Leaf Clover
Barbara Acklin - Love Makes A Woman
Barbara Lynn - You Make Me So Hot
Barbara Mason - World In A Crisis
Bar-Kays - Feels Like I'm Falling In Love
Barry White - Midnight And You, Come On, I'm Gonna
Love You Just A Little Bit More Baby, Its Only Love
Doing It's Thing, September When I First Met You
Ben E. King - Street Tough, Spoiled
Betty Wright - Smother Me With Your Love, We Down,
Clean Up Woman (Extended Version), After The Pain
Bill Brandon - The Streets Got My Lady
Bill Harris - Am I Cold, Am I Hot

Bill Withers - Make Love To Your Mind
Billy Griffin - Hold Me Tighter In The Rain
Black Ice - Postcard Love Affair
Bob & Gene - It's Not What You Know (It's Who You Know)
Bobbi Humphrey - Baby Don't You Know, Sunset Burgundy
Bobby Glover - Bright Skies, Sunny Days, It's My Turn, Happy
Bobby Womack - How Could You Break My Heart
Bottom & Company - Gonna Find A True Love
Breakwater - Say You Love Me Girl
Breakwater - Work It Out
Brenda & Herb - What Goes Around
Brenda Holloway - You've Made Me So Very Happy, My Baby Moves Me, A Little Bit Of Love
Cameo - Love You Anyway
Camiel - Trying To Get To You
Candi Staton - Young Hearts Run Free
Candy Bowman - Since I Found You
Geraldine Hunt - Can't Fake The Feeling
Carl Anderson - Buttercup
Incognito & Carleen Anderson - Trouble Don't Last Always
Carrie Lucas With The Whispers - Hello Stranger
Cecil Parker - Really Really Love You
Chuck Mangione - Do You Ever Think About Me
Coke Escovedo - I Wouldn't Change A Thing
Collage - When You Smile
Maceo & The Macks - Cross The Track (We Batter Go Back)

Crusaders - Street Life
Curtis Mayfield - Tripping Out
D.J. Rodgers - Secret Lady
D'Angelo - Girl You Need A Change Of Mind
Viola Wills - Dare To Dream
David Ruffin & Eddie Kendrick - Don't Know Why You're Dreaming
Dayton - Promise Me, The Sound Of Music
Dee Edwards - I Can Deal With That
The Deele - Two Occasions
Benny Golson - I'm Always Dancing To The Music
Diana Ross - It's My House
Don Blackman - Holding You, Loving You
Donald Byrd - Places And Spaces
Donna McGhee - It Aint No Big Thing
Double Exposure - My Love Is Free
Dr Hook - Sexy Eyes
Dynasty - Adventures In The Land Of Music
Earth, Wind & Fire - On Your Face, The One
Eddie Harris - It's All Right Now
Edna Wright - Oops! Here I Go Again
Eighties Ladies - Turned On To You
Esther Phillips - I Hope You'll Be Very Unhappy Without Me
Santiago - Feeling Good
Foster Sylvers - Misdemeanor
Four Tops - Strung Out For Your Love
Maze Featuring Frankie Beverly - Silky Soul
Galaxxy - Spend Some Time
Gene Dunlap Featuring The Ridgeways - Before You Break My Heart

Genobia Jeter - All Of My Love
George Benson - Breezin'
George Duke - I Want you For Myself, Look What You Find
Greg Perry - Variety Is The Spice Of Life
Gwen McCrae - 90% Of Me Is You
The Isley Brothers - Harvest For The World
Harvey Mason - Till You Take My Love
Heatwave - Super Soul Sister
Herbie Hancock - I Thought It Was You
Hi Rhythm - On The Loose
Hi -Tension - There's A Reason
Hugh Masakela - Ibala Lam
I - Level - In The Sand
Quincy Jones Featuring The Brothers Johnson - Is It Love That We're Missin'
Jackie Wilson - I Don't Want To Lose You, I Get The Sweetest Feeling
Michael Jackson - I Wanna Be Where You Are
Jean Carn - Don't Let It Go To Your Head
Jean Knight - Mr. Big Stuff
Jeffree - Love's Gonna Last
Jennifer Hudson - Love You I Do
Jermaine Jackson - You Like Me Don't You
Jill Francis - Make Love To Me
John & Arthur Simms - Love Will Getcha'
Johnny Hammond - Tell Me What To Do
Josie James - Win Your Love
Kenny Lattimore - Never Too Busy, Right Down To It, Come To Me, Destiny
Kenny Loggins - This Is It

L A Boppers – You Did It Good
Leon Ware – Rockin' You Eternally
Leroy Hudson – It's Different
Groove Collective – Lift Off
Linda Clifford – Runaway Love
Linda Williams – Elevate Our Minds
Lou Rawls – You'll Never Find Another Love Like Mine
Foxy – Madamoiselle
Marvin Gaye – Let's Get It On, What's Going On
Matt Covington – We Got One
Maxi – Lover To Lover
Mayer Hawthorne – The Walk
Maze Featuring Frankie Beverly – Before I Let You Go,
Joy And Pain
McGhee – Now That I Have You
M.C.B – Time Is Right
Melvin Hudson – Life In The City
Michael Henderson – Take Me I'm Yours
The Jacksons – Blues Away
Michael McDonald – I Keep Forgettin'
Milton Wright – Keep It Up
Minnie Ripperton – Back Down Memory Lane
Natalie Cole – This Will Be (An Everlasting Love)
Natural High – I Think I'm Falling In Love With You
Norman Connors – Be There In The Morning
Norman Connors Featuring Glen Jones – Sing A Love
Song
O'Bryan – Doin' Alright
Phyllis Hyman – What You Won't Do For Love
Pleasure – Let Me Be The One, Nothin' To It, Glide
Plustwo – Stop Fantasy

Plush - We've Got The Love
Point 3 FM - Picks Me Up (Your Love)
Positive Force - Give You My Love
Quincy Jones - Heaven's Girl, Human Nature
R. Kelly - Share My Love
Kathy Buck - Don't Beat Around The Bush
Real Thing - You To Me Are Everything
Reel People Featuring Dyanna Fearon - Butterflies
Reel People Featuring Angela Johnson - Cant Stop
Rene & Angela - Imaginary Playmates
Richard 'Dimples' Field - I Like Your Loving, If It Ain't
One Thing Its Another
Richard Tee - That's The Way Of The World
Ripple - I Don't Know What It Is But It Sure Is Funky
Roberta Flack & Donny Hathaway - Back Together
Again
Roger - I Want To Be Your Man
Rose Banks - You're Much Too Beautiful For Words
Roy Ayers - Searching
Roy Ayers Ubiquity - Everybody Loves The Sunshine
Epicenter Featuring Sandra Feva - You Can't Come
Up In Here No More
Sergio Mendes And Brasil 77 - The Waters Of March
(Aguas De Março)
Shakatak - Easier Said Than Done
The Vibrations - Shake It Up
Sharon Jones & the Dap-Kings - Take Me With U
Side Effect - Keep That Same Old Feeling, Midnight
Lover, Private World, S.O.S
Sinclair - I Want You Back
Solo - Heaven

Sonya Spence - Let Love Flow On
Soul Survivors - City Of Brotherly Love
Splendor - Special Lady
Starvue - Body Fusion
Mandrill - Stay Tonite
Stephanie Mills Featuring Teddy Pendergrass - Two Hearts
Steve Parks - Movin' In The Right Direction
Stevie Wonder - Master Blaster (Jammin')
Sugar Hill Gang - Passion Play
Switch - There'll Never Be, I Call Your Name
Syleena Johnson - Guess What, I Am Your Woman
Sylvia Striplin - You Can't Turn Me Away
Tavares - I Hope You'll Be Very Unhappy Without Me, Never Had A Love Like This Before
Teddy Pendergrass - When Somebody Loves You Back, It's Time For Love
Ten City - Put Love Where You Want It
The Wells - Who's That Stranger
The Blackbyrds - Walking In Rhythm
The Caprells - What You Need Baby
The Emotions - Don't Ask My Neighbours, Layedd Back, Rejoice, Blessed
The Futures - Ain't No Time Fa Nothing
The Gap Band - Yearning For Your Love
Jackson Five - ABC
The Jacksons - This Place Hotel
The Jones Girls - Dance Turned To A Romance
The Lovelites - Love So Strong
The Main Ingredient - Work To Do
The McCrarys - Love On A Summer Night

The O'Jays – We're All In This Thing Together
The Quotations - I Don't Have To Worry
The Radiants - It Ain't No Big Thing
The System – Heaven In Your Eyes
The Two Tons - Never Like This
The Vibrations - Shake It Up
The Whispers - (Olivia) Lost And Turned Out
Isaac Hayes - Theme From Shaft
Tony Troutman - What's The Use
Valentine Brothers –This Kind Of Love (Is So Special)
Vanessa Kendrick - 90% Of Me Is You
Vernon Birch - Lovely Lady
Vicki Anderson - The Message From The Soul Sisters
Weapons Of Peace - Just Keep On Smiling
Wendy Walker - We've Got One
Whitney Houston - My Heart Is Calling
Willie Beaver Hale - Groove-On, Hale - Let The Good
Times Roll
Willie Bobo - Comin' Over Me
Willie Hutch - Easy Does It
Womack & Womack – Baby I'm Scared Of You
Young Holt Unlimited - Soulful Strut
Barbara Acklin - Am I The Same Girl
Yvonne Gage - Tonight (I Wanna Love You)

RACE, AWARENESS & TRAINING

Defenders of the Doctrine

The importance of the following events marks the beginning of a phase in my life that I would rather not have experienced. The shadow and impact of racism created a large cloud over my carefree and happy-go-lucky life.

In 1973, Gibson Road Church organised a visit to the seaside for the day. We all arrived early at Church that morning in order to catch the coach. The food and drink circulated and everyone was in a boisterous mood anticipating the fun of the fair and chilling by the sea front. On arrival, we were briefed on what time to return to the coach for departure back to Birmingham the same day. We were told that it would be alright to leave our belongings on the coach, because it would be open all day.

Whilst my group were in a games arcade, we ran into another group from the church, but instead of having fun they were in total panic mode. I knew there were problems straight away. They told us that white gangs had been attacking black people along the main promenade and they were trying to get back to the coach. When we left the arcade we headed towards the main fairground and went on the bumper cars. Suddenly, Deacon Martin appeared; he was clearly alarmed and demanded that we all make our way back to the coach immediately. Apparently, the report by the earlier group was true and there had been several attacks on blacks over the last couple of hours.

When we eventually arrived back at the coach, the driver wasn't there, which meant we wouldn't be going anywhere. Obviously, everybody was talking about the reports of the racist attacks but there were some who tried to dismiss it as pure rumour and conjecture. In order to lighten the mood, fried chicken that been prepared was being dished out. Black people always find comfort in food – especially chicken. Suddenly, one of the brothers came onto the coach in a panic and said that the white people were coming. A few hundred skinheads appeared, looking for blacks to attack. They were walking towards the coach park where we were on the coach without a driver. The skinheads stopped in front of the coach and started clapping, chanting their racist chants and performing their Nazi style salutes. More white people arrived and it was almost as if the gates had been opened at the end of a local football match. It seemed as though we were all going to die and there was a sense of impending doom as there were so many skinheads.

Panic swept through the coach like the Holy Spirit in the Church. The women hurriedly packed away the food packages and the serving implements became potential weapons to be used as a last resort in self-defence. The younger children were moved towards the back of the coach and the men disembarked and dismantled a lorry that was parked next to the coach taking anything that would serve as a weapon. The men stood like soldiers ready to defend us against the overwhelming and increasing number of skinheads that stood in front of the besieged coach – the same men who sat in church every Sunday to worship white Jesus, were now confronted with what felt like a throwback to slavery days. Why did these white boys want to injure us? The group was mainly mothers and children. The men were brave but they would not have stood a chance against the skinhead mob - we would have been overcome and overturned in seconds.

I'm not sure exactly whose idea it was, but a few of us decided to get off the coach despite mummy and the other women trying to stop us. Watching your son defend against the racist Klan is not something any mum wants to see. Can you imagine their pain right then? At that moment there was no obvious threat at the back of the coach so we left via the rear exit. We could see traffic on the other side of the car park so we ran in that direction hoping to find a policeman or someone who could alert the police for us. It took some time to find 'a bobby on the beat' and when we approached him, we were all shouting at once. He held up his hands to calm us down and then asked us to speak one at a time. One of us blurted out what was happening at the coach park. We ran back, assuming he had radioed for back-up and were able to reassure the women that we had told the police and that they would arriving immediately.

Outside the coach, the clapping and singing reached fever pitch and the tension was palpable. The men continued to stand steadfast in front of the coach, determined to protect the women and children.

Suddenly, the piercing sound of police sirens could be heard and policemen were arriving on foot from across the car park. A great sense of relief was felt by everyone; the women started clapping and the men returned to the coach placing their weapons back onto the lorry as they filed past. Everyone burst into spontaneous applause and song. At last the thugs had been dispersed - I have never known any other time when black people were happy to see the police!

Amazingly, as if from nowhere, the driver suddenly returned to the coach and we quickly left. Yep, for sure Jesus saved us that day from a fate that would have dealt a fatal blow. It was some time before any further trips were organised.

Great Barr Comprehensive School

In 1972, whilst still at junior school I used to go to watch my brother play Rugby on Saturday mornings at his new school. Great Barr Comprehensive School was one of the largest schools in the country with as many as a thousand students. When it was my turn to attend that school, I found out what it meant to be black as there were only fifty or so black students among the whole school population and only one black teacher. Mr Ramos, a podgy, bearded but formidable Caribbean gentleman had a very eloquent Caribbean undertone in his accent. He was an absolute cricket fanatic and of course the West Indies were invincible at the time.

On my way to school on the first day, I met a guy named Peter Bent at the bus stop. He was a large burly 'red skinned' guy with a beaming smile and we immediately became 'home boys'. Peter lived on Westminster Road and was pretty much the same size as me and his family came from St Elizabeth, Jamaica, the same as my dad's family. Peter's mother is Mr Swaby's (from Mansfield Road) sister. Peter talked nonstop and there was never a dull moment with him - he was eleven, going on sixteen. He had two older brothers, Dwain and Claude, and like me, Peter was accessing things that kids our age should not have been.

'Racism' 101

My first day at Great Barr was the day I personally experienced racism from a class mate. A white guy called Steven sat in front of me in the classroom. Barely five minutes had passed before the jesting began. Steven spun around on his chair and faced me saying *"All white mate? Wog's the matter? Nigger mind, you coon... Sunshine"* and other derogatory racist phrases. Rocking back in my chair and remaining silent, the barrage of abuse continued with accompanying laughter and jeering from other white boys sitting around my desk. Then I heard a voice say *"leave him alone"* which came from the girl sitting to my left who was a good looking if slightly plumpish white girl with long dark hair and 'Chiny looking eyes'. Her name was Katie and she alone stepped up and tackled the racist Steven about his behaviour towards me. He laughed, dismissed her and told her to shut up. However, she was determined to admonish him for his actions. For the first time I thought maybe it wasn't going to be all bad.

I have never forgotten this small but selfless act by Katie and I have always been thankful to her although we never became friends at school. Katie was the one dissenting voice in the classroom. The teacher's attempts to manage the disruption rather than deal with Steven's racist behaviour left me powerless. I thought to myself, is this what I have to look forward to - getting racially abused on a daily basis? I sat there quietly smiling, the way black boys do when they don't fully comprehend, as Marvin Gaye would say, *'what's going on'*. The racist behaviour continued for the duration of what was my first form period which, as you can imagine, seemed to last forever. I was, trapped in a room with people that just did not like me and furthermore, they were allowed to be vocal about it. The teacher did manage to say *"now come on lads calm down"*, a few times but did not actually stop the activity.

The wait for the break time bell felt like an eternity – I had no protection from the racist abuse. For me, that bell would signal my release and enable me to go and find my brother, 'Blackeye', and 'Saddo' Barber. In anticipation of break time, I searched through my pockets to find coins my mum had given me to buy snacks if needed. I took out a fifty pence piece and placed it on the desk whilst putting my text book into my bag. Suddenly Steven, the racist, grabbed the coin off the desk and, grasping it tightly, placed it into his trouser pocket.

Putting down my bag, I told Steven to put my money back down on the desk and go about his business. The school bell finally rang indicating break time so I asked him again to return my money to me. He then started to swear at me and was about to call me a wog. At this point, I grabbed him around his throat and threw him backwards against a cupboard at the front of the class. Striking him hard in the stomach with my right hand, I held him around his neck with my left hand. The teacher intervened and tried to prise my hand from around his throat. Strangely the teacher did not try to prevent the abuse targeted at me, but chose to protect the racists when they faced the consequences of their actions. I stood emotionless and wouldn't release my grip, saying "I want my money back" "he's taken my money". Eventually, Steven dropped my coin to the floor which rolled around by his feet, proving to the teacher that I was telling the truth.

Bishop, who was in my class, was another overt racist. He was part of a gang that was tagged the 'Tower Hill Mob' and he seemed to believe that he was the chief spokesperson for the white race. Although he wasn't involved in the initial skirmish in the classroom, he soon made himself known to me. Bishop was a chicken and on his own, he was nothing. However, as part of a white terrorist group he posed more of a threat. He claimed he would call his Aryan brothers to create problems for me on a daily basis and one of his brothers was called Tony. Tony was reputed to be something of a hooligan and would regularly attempt to intimidate and threaten me with assault by his gang. He was the sort that had a pair of high-top Doc Marten boots and dressed in braces and three-quarter length jeans. He was obnoxious and irritating and there were many times when I wanted to slap him so hard but stopped myself. He just wasn't worth it. Starting battles would never be straightforward because anyone involved would have to consider the probable response to any action against blacks. Brawls with white biker gangs who sought to assault black students outside the school grounds were a common occurrence. The racists scorned me solely because of the colour of my skin. Moore and Bishop had a bully mentality and were racists with evil minds.

There was one occasion after a basketball match when we, the black boys, left the upper school gym and there outside on the playground, were approximately forty bikers. We were instructed to return to the gym, whilst the rugby teacher attempted to disperse the mob. We ran towards the Dyas Road entrance gate as we knew their bikes would not be able to get through, hoping that decision would allow us to catch a bus before they got around to the streets. We were wrong, there wasn't a bus so we ran from Great Barr School all the way back to Perry Barr. We jumped into front gardens and hid as the bike gang circled, looking for us. Words cannot explain the sense of relief that we felt when we eventually reached the roundabout at Perry Barr and ran down Aston Lane.

Running away from racist bullies was a regular occurrence. After school one winter's day, I caught the early bus to Perry Barr Library and as the bus approached my stop I got up and walked downstairs. In front of me waiting to get off was a white man, and outside the bus a group of black boys were waiting at the bus shelter. As soon as the bus doors opened they let fly a torrent of snow balls and unfortunately, the white man received the full brunt of it. The perpetrators ran off around the corner with the man in pursuit and I got off the bus and walked towards the library. Hearing a man shouting racial profanities, I looked around and saw it was the man from the bus who by now was running towards me. Throwing up both of my hands, I explained that I was not involved and that I had been on the bus standing behind him. However, he was not listening and kept coming towards me, gesturing wildly with his arms.

This crazy white man chased me and stupidly I thought I would be safe inside the library as there would be no chance of anyone attacking me there. I was wrong! Following me into the library, the man went on to 'batter' me in front of library staff. Grabbing me, he held me by my collar whilst he hit me several times with his free hand. Throwing me into one bookcase after another, he continued to punch me several times in the stomach and kidney area whilst calling me lots of variations on 'nigger' and 'wog'. His attempts to punch me in the face mainly failed as I raised my hands to block them. I was 13 years old and a grown white man with a big moustache had laid into me without remorse.

Feeling a sense of relief at being with my own black crew, it felt safe to get on with normal break time activity. Black boys tended to stay together in one area of the playground. Everyone spoke to one another - there were no outsiders. Some of the older guys had attended my junior school and for those who didn't already know me I was introduced as "Charlie's brother, Owen." Black kids had to stick together for safety from the white racist ambushes that were targeting lone black kids. Aston life was a million miles away from life in what felt to me like a prison with black inmates and white guards. It was hard not to become militant after suffering the racism that we endured on a daily basis.

There were some days when race relations were worse than normal; usually after there had been a skirmish or assault on someone and then at break time the whole playground would split in two. All the blacks were on one side of the yard and the whites on the other. It was always the white boys intent on enraging us as they made monkey noises and shouted racial abuse. The nature of a coward is to agitate from the back of the crowd, hiding behind others as they too shout abuse. Putting it simply, blacks never instigated these activities. They were always initiated by white hooligans.

Rarely was there a spontaneous fight which would be over and done with. Generally it would be arranged to take place during break time attracting the attention of haters as well as non-haters. However, the partition of the playground forced you to stand on one side or the other, as though both groups were literally gangs. Let me put this into context for you.

I remember always having to be vigilant and to look out for the other black guys who chilled together. It became quite normal for the black guys to wait and roam together.

Sometimes We are All Mixed Up

Richard was in my form and joined the class halfway through the year. He was mixed race and a lot more palatable to the average white boy in the class than I was. He was short, with a small afro and was quite popular amongst the white boys. However, that changed whenever the playground split. Richard would go over to the side where the white boys stood, expecting to be accepted, because in Richard's opinion, he was not black. The bullies, however, thought he was black enough and Richard could be heard shouting "my mother is white" as they begun to pound him.

Mixed race people may or may not be aware of the privilege they are afforded over that of a black person and, as such, unconsciously condone the treatment of black people by the system. The view that 'my mother is white' or my 'father is white' can be manipulated to suit the occasion. Mixed race privilege is also abused because mixed race people are, on occasion, willing to use their privileges only for themselves. People who are aware of the problem and recognise what white privilege means, are more able to point out the injustice and can influence both black and white.

The issues faced by young blacks in school were not only about the actual fights but the reluctance and the 'turning a blind eye' which was systematic in the school culture. These incidents of racial terrorism and vile behaviour were attempts to humiliate and degrade blacks in the school. These kinds of experiences breed a new kind of animal, one that decides that 'no one is ever going to do this to me again'. So, there comes a time when a man has to learn to deal with his own business, and survive out there whatever happens. A man can't be a man if he allows himself to be humiliated by racists.

"When children attend schools that place a greater value on discipline and security than on intellectual development, they are attending prep school for prison." **Angela Davis.**

The Sum of all Fears

My concerns weren't about the beating that I had just received, but explaining and convincing my parents that the bruises were as a result of being beaten up by white people. I am convinced Jamaican parents do not know how to respond to crisis involving their children. They have practised and perfected the art of absolute denial in contrast to supporting other black victims of any traumatic experience. The most comfortable position for Jamaican parents is always to blame their child or the victim. They simply didn't believe that things happened to people who did not do anything wrong. In fact, it was easier for a Jamaican to beat you up, on top of your existing injuries, for having let it happen to you in the first place.

"It is easier to build strong children rather than broken men." **Frederick Douglas**

The Black Man's Champion – The Right Honourable 'Saddo' Barber

Some of the black guys were real tough guys but the absolute 'King of Crazy' was 'Saddo' Barber. 'Saddo' was and had always been crazy from junior school. One day he had a fight with a guy called Gary. Gary's family were one of the last white families in Aston and like many of us, Gary ended up at Great Barr. Attending Great Barr was a cultural shock for him because when he was at junior school, he was the minority and at secondary school he was a part of the majority. Because Gary was familiar with the black guys from Aston he believed that he would be allowed to suddenly behave like the whites at Great Barr. These guys were three years older than me and I only got wind of the fight on the grapevine as rumours circulated throughout the school all day. Everyone knew 'Saddo' was crazy and it was a bruising and violent fight that went on for some time before he nearly pounded the life out of Gary. It was a high price for Gary to pay to gain acceptance into the racist gangs of the school.

Whilst sitting in the changing room, bantering after a basketball match, 'Saddo' put on a performance for the troops whilst we waited for everyone to be ready to go home after school. He decided that he would demonstrate his strength by attempting to pick me up from my seat. (Bearing in mind that this was the second week of school and my uniform was brand spanking new). Before I could escape, he grabbed hold of me by my blazer collars and adjusted his flat feet to get a firm stance to lift me from the seat. By the time I realised his plan it was too late for me to move out of the way as he had already grabbed hold of me. Helplessly sitting there, with my blazer pressing into my armpits, and my view obscured by the expression on 'Saddo's' face as he strained to pull my blazer upwards, I was like a race horse with blinkers on - with only a view of his big head, closed eyes, flaring nostrils, and big lips as his facial expression contorted under my weight. Any sensible person would know that the seams in the blazer would give way. The blazer ripped from my back and with a massive release of pressure, which threw 'Saddo's' arms upwards, the remnants of my brand-new blazer were revealed.

The changing room fell silent as everyone stared at us and then spontaneous outbursts of laughter began. People were delirious as I remained sitting on the bench unmoved by the lifting process. 'Saddo' found it hilarious, rolling around on the floor clutching his stomach. I saw the funny side of that moment and laughed along with everyone else. I grabbed the shreds of my new blazer out of his hands before he could do any further damage to it. In the midst of the laughter 'Saddo' started calling me 'Hulk'. From that single incident, the tag 'Hulk' was born.

The other side of this story was that my mother did not find it funny at all. After showing her the blazer when I got home, she went berserk and instinctively attacked me with a few quick head shots and threatened me with every form of violence known to man. Then she cooled down and cussed me for about half an hour, whilst she sorted out the food. Then fed me. As the old saying goes, 'after the storm, there must be a calm.'

The following morning I wondered how I was going to go to school without my blazer. I thought that my mum would purchase a brand new blazer, so that I would have no problems with authority at school. Oh no! Not my mum! When I got ready for school and put on my blazer, I was shocked. Mum had repaired it but with the thread showing on the outside and I had to wear it for the whole year! In my father's house there may be many mansions, but you only get one school uniform and one pair of school shoes which had to last the whole year - that was the rule.

On another occasion, 'Saddo' was arguing in the changing room with the rugby teacher, who was bigger than most and not really the kind of person to mess around with. But 'Saddo' would never back down from anyone, especially a white man. It wasn't long before the rugby teacher had enough of him and decided to eject him from the changing room/gym area. 'Saddo' was told to not only leave the gym but to go home immediately. Naturally, he responded badly to this proposition. But the rugby teacher wasn't joking and 'Saddo' wasn't leaving. 'Saddo' continued to argue with the rugby teacher who eventually pushed him out, like a rag doll. It was a comfort to know that 'Saddo' was at Great Barr. His fighting spirit enabled him to represent all blacks in the school and he was at the forefront of all the fights which took place in Perry Barr Park – he was a defender of the black boys and 'Saddo' was the one who had our back in any fight situation.

Coded Message in Alex Hayley's 'Roots'

In 1977, there was a definite a buzz amongst the youths on Freer Road. A great deal of excitement and anticipation was in the air about the televising of *Roots*. Even people who didn't usually watch TV showed enthusiasm.

The televising of *Roots* was the first time that anyone decided to make known our history. We all sat around to watch this programme; and from the very first clip the room fell silent. Everybody stared at the screen, for once there were no questions being asked by my mum, as was the norm when attempting to watch television. I connected with *Roots* totally but I don't think that my mum connected with the African element, even though the actors were American. She strenuously denies being African. I wept.

Roots revealed to me for the first time the horrors that black people had endured. It provided an insight into how life must have been for my ancestors and what my own grandparents, great grandparents and all those before them had to endure. Until the televising of *Roots*, the only programmes shown on UK television that had black people in were *Tarzan*, *Rising Damp* and *Love Thy Neighbour*. Occasionally, a documentary or reports of famine in Africa would be shown and those proved ironically useful in encouraging UK blacks to disassociate with

Africa and African-ness. Also, it was impossible to comprehend the nightmarish images of lynching, beating, oppression, slavery. We were not taught this in school and black youths felt that the truth had now been revealed and proved that black people were oppressed.

The Art of War (Fighting without Fighting)

Great Barr School had successfully managed to teach me that as black men in this society we need to be able to defend ourselves, our family and those few rights afforded to us as a community. Therefore learning to fight was mandatory. Since school I had wanted to learn karate and how to defend myself properly but my mother was firmly against that idea, to anything that got me involved in violence. So it was not until after I left school that it became possible to join karate class to harness my innate fighting skills.

In those days there was a new phenomenon known as Bruce Lee who gained international fame from audiences with his unique brand of martial arts on films coming America instead of out of China. In Handsworth, a well known martial artist called 'Captain Boogie' set up a film night at the Elite cinema on Soho Road. Three films were shown each night beginning at midnight until the early hours of the morning. The inspirational idea quickly took a hold amongst young blacks and quite soon Friday night officially became kung fu night.

The building housing the cinema had seen better days and was run-down, dirty and depressing. However, in the dark and once the films started, the surroundings and conditions did not detract from the thrills on the big screen. There would be hundreds of guys lined up waiting to get into the cinema and at the front of the queue there was only one security man at the box office. Normally this would be a recipe for a disaster, as everyone would rush the security man and get in. But it seemed the Captain's presence alone stopped that sort of behaviour before it started. It seemed as though everyone knew him, Blacks, Asians and Whites alike and when grasping his hand everyone treated him with total reverence in an almost Godfather-like way.

He entertained everyone as he paced up and down greeting people in the queue. Eton and Ivor already knew the 'Captain' and they told me "it's Natty and Carol dem brother". We went to Broadway with three Pinkneys so the stories of the family were already legendary. After greeting the 'Captain', Eton and Ivor introduced me to him. As soon as they told him my name, like most people, he shouted out **"HULK!"** and burst into laughter, commenting on how well the name suited me by saying, *"Yeah man, you're de real Hulk man"*. He extended his hand to grasp mine, and remarked on my size as he peered upward above me towards the sky. His whole manner and composure enamoured me towards him. He was very buoyant and moved with grace and elegance turning almost in a pirouette like style, whilst he looked out occasionally to monitor the queue or shout encouragement to people. He was the most entertaining doorman I'd ever seen. I got to know the 'Captain' pretty well; he was genuine, full of tricks, fun and enthusiastic.

Attending Great Barr School made me want to learn karate, but my mum's protective nature prevented me from going along to a class. However, having left school I was free to start. 'Captain Boogie' (Hector Pinkney) is an infamous character and was one of the local martial art heroes in the early 1980s. He arrived in the UK from Jamaica in 1962 to join his mother Mavis. She tried to develop an initiative to keep good values within the community and campaigned to build the Muhammad Ali Centre in Hockley. Sadly, we lost the 'Great Lady' in the 1980s and 'Captain Boogie' has continued to follow in his mother's footsteps, working tirelessly to realise her dream. The 'Captain' had been a student of the infamous Beenie Brown's Karate School at 104 Heathfield Road which focused on empowering black men in self defence. The 'Captain' had excelled as Beenie's student and moved on to establish his own karate school. The 'action hero' had not yet been invented for TV screens in the late 70s and early 80s so Kung Fu night at Elite Cinema offered a new and exciting form of fighting that never ever failed to thrill.

Dojo Karate Club

The 'Captain' told me that that he had a club and invited me to join and learn karate with him. The following Wednesday, after group rehearsal had finished, I rushed to my first session. I arrived slightly late and the sparring had already started. There were eight or nine students training with the 'Captain' and my initial session merely proved that it was physically possible for me to become as good as those students. Putting in the necessary work to learn the skills that the 'Captain' displayed was something that I was determined to do.

As youths we threw our legs around in a kick-like motion which appeared to be the same as Bruce Lee's. However, they were nothing like Bruce's! It didn't matter what type of kick I attempted, they were all pretty awful in comparison to those used by the other students in the class. But through sheer determination over a few months, my techniques improved and more people joined the class.

The 'Captain' introduced different martial arts instructors who dusted off their Gis and assisted at the sessions. There was Master Ray a student of Lau Gar kung fu, Master Errol from Shotokan (zen shin), and from wada rye karate came Sensei Tullo and Bailey. Each week, they took it in turns to deliver sessions teaching the elements from their own style which the students enjoyed immensely. Not only did I show significant improvement in all the styles that were taught to us, but my flexibility also substantively improved and I was inches away from achieving the full splits. The 'Captain's' own martial art style was a combination of several techniques. He taught us to learn any technique and how to apply the technique in a fight.

My reputation outside the Dojo began to increase and people who were involved in martial arts and also knew the 'Captain', would stop me to 'big me up'. I assume that he told other people about my antics in his class, and it wasn't long before his class became the spot where people would come to watch the fights. Pretty soon, there were experienced fighters from other clubs showing up at the classes each week with the sole intention of fighting me.

Being a relative beginner, I only had a white belt which came in the bag with my karate suit and many of the challengers were experienced brown and black belts – but they only came to fight me. The fighting got more intense each week but my sheer size, strength and athleticism, together with the mastering of a few new techniques, elevated me to top fighter and I won all my fights. Then it dawned on me that fighting came as naturally to me as rugby and basketball. Running for my life from the racist gangs from Great Barr School had paid dividends as I was already fearless; and coupled with formal training I was a formidable opponent for any fighter.

First Tournament

Other than on the big screen, I had never seen or been to a tournament. We arrived dressed like TV characters: 'Eastman' wore a white Gi with the sleeves cut off at the shoulder and a pair of black Gi bottoms and I paid to have an elaborate black and red and kung fu suit made in China Town.

Surprisingly, there were a lot of guys from Aston who looked efficient and official. I met Fred Rose, the head of the Great Britain Karate Federation, for the first time. Everyone came over and greeted the 'Captain' whilst he bobbed around and introduced us saying that he wanted to give the team some experience. The time soon came for my first Kumite, (first fight) which was against a white guy, a purple belt. The referee said 'Ajjimay' (start) and I moved forward to engage my opponent. He slipped aside and moved out of my strike range using his ring craft to get around the mat and was obviously trying to assess my capability before attempting to strike me. As he moved to try a cheap head shot, I delivered a Mia-geri kick straight into his midriff area. The guy screamed as he fell backward and began vomiting. He landed on the mat a couple of feet from where he had started to punch. He was hardly moving and people rushed over to him - he was clearly hurt. I stood there on my mark waiting for the result of the fight to be delivered by the referee and was nearly disqualified for hitting too hard. Fortunately, my opponent was alright and I progressed in the tournament.

All of my following fights in the tournament were watched by the other competitors. The black belts from other clubs shook my hands and said that they were glad that they did not have to fight me. From that day forwards, the Dojo Karate Club had 'a name' on the circuit and 'Captain Boogie' was recognised for his club. The rest of the team also did really well in their bouts.

During the coming months, my focus became learning sport karate which unlike karate is a 'non contact' sport.

Pay Back

Keith Copeland, aka 'the mouth of Aston', wanted to train with me. This was a perfect opportunity for me to get revenge for him whipping my brother and bullying us. This was going to be a fight where no one could run as I anticipated that he would either go crazy or complain about the outcome, should he lose.

Keith was an exponent of Shotakan style karate and we agreed to spar in his back garden. However, his preference was to do a full workout with only an element of sparring. This was fine with me. We started with stretching but it wasn't long before Keith began to complain and make excuses: for example that he *hadn't trained properly for some time.*' By the time we actually started sparring, it was clear that Keith was no longer at his best and that he could be easily subdued. Every time I hit him, he walked off around the garden shouting. By the end of that day, I was finally free of the demon in me that had wanted to punish him for his intimidating behaviour towards my brother and me all those years ago.

Sensei Jerome was the best known wada ryu karate fighter in Aston. We already knew each other from Prince Albert Junior School. He was part of what was, at the time, a massive crew of black guys from Aston who were studying martial arts at Temple in Birmingham City Centre. Jerome trained with the great Jeff Douglas at Temple before sadly, Aston lost the internationally renowned martial artist, icon, teacher, fighter and all-around good guy in the early 70s. Therefore, Jerome was as close to the Japanese source as I could get at the time.

I attended his club with the sole purpose of acquiring the skills needed to obtain a black belt. Being young, rude, cocky and confident, not only did I ask him to teach me, but also insulted him by asserting that I was better than him.

We stepped onto the mat for a sparring session and within a few seconds he was holding my slumped body in his arms as he had caught me before I hit the mat. He is the only person to have ever knocked me flat out and he did it with such skill, speed and control that I could only beg him to allow me to be his student thereafter.

Sensei Jerome was a quietly spoken Rasta man with long 'natty dread', who actively helped and supported me in learning karate. He was a formidable fighter without question and I studied diligently with Sensei for a few months before taking on formal wada rye grading with the Great Britain Karate Federation. I was still attending training with my mentor, the 'Captain', and endeavoured to share all my learning with the students at Dojo club.

Those days heralded the arrival of a new enemy in our community from America - crack cocaine. Crack cocaine decimated the future and potential of many youths, particularly from Aston, and unfortunately my great master teacher became a victim of this abhorrent drug. Local hoodlums viciously attacked him because he was hopelessly hooked on crack. He lost his ability to function and he sustained severe injuries as he took those beatings.

This great man was reduced to a shell of his former self. He was one of the many 'crack babies' that the drug gave birth to in our community. It was an epidemic that swept through our young people making perfectly normal people become totally dysfunctional, who didn't live, but rather existed for the sole purpose of serving their addiction to the drug.

Security Work

The 'Captain' held a blues party at his mum's house and asked me to do the security. People came from all over Birmingham and there were lots of 'big man dem.' All was well until after midnight when a group of approximately 10 local youths arrived, insisting that they walk in without paying and threatening to 'rush' me. Standing firm and not moving from the doorway, I spread my arms out touching each wall and dug in, whilst the youths attempted to get past me from both sides. It was like a rugby scrum which went on for a few minutes before they gave up. After five years playing a prop forward, this was not new to me. The onlookers, who stood in the hallway behind me, started praising me, amazed that none of the youths had gained entry. People laughed at how 'Hulk' had stopped the posse. Everyone unanimously decided that I was 'the top doorman'. I had prevented the youths from getting in with a minimum of fuss, ensuring that blood was shed and nobody's life had been taken. At the time, I was not aware that the youths were a notorious posse who were well known in the area and it later dawned on me that things could have got quite serious. The youths never forgot my name, 'Hulk', and always took the time to greet me and reminisce about that night.

Whilst at 'Captain Boogie's' blues party, I was approached by a club owner who spoke to me about the possibility of more door work at the notorious Night Spot on Lozells Road. He offered me the role as doorman every Saturday night and I grabbed the opportunity with both hands.

Night Spot was the place where the most toughened gangland members would pass through during the course of the night. I worked there for a year and never encountered any problems on the door. I was surrounded by doormen, who always seemed to be aggressive with the clientele, but I had a completely different approach, always seeking to maintain peace. The other doormen would challenge the clients over simple things. Being polite at all times was a must for me as it made the clients feel safe rather than hassled. The major difference between me and the doormen I worked with was that I was a disciplined martial arts fighter. I soon got door work at Tabasco and then Verlie's night club and the Hummingbird night club in the city centre. Arguably, I think my most enjoyable door job was working the Porsche Club in Small Heath. Pay could easily be negotiated as a doorman with the black clubs and one hundred pounds per night could be made by working on just one door. If a doorman had a good reputation, then it was possible to get hired for a blues after a club finished at 2am until 6am. It was easy to make two hundred pounds in one night.

Ready for the Fight - Birmingham Show

'Skipper' never attended karate training with us, although he had been invited by me on numerous occasions. One night he returned from the Birmingham show and his mouth was badly cut and bleeding. He explained that he had been walking down the road with a group of Broadway men when they noticed a guy running towards them from the opposite direction. They ignored him as he didn't appear threatening and carried on talking amongst themselves. As he passed, he punched 'Skipper' squarely in his mouth and carried on running. 'Skipper's' lip exploded. Too shocked to react straight away, by the time they did the guy was some distance away from them, still running. 'Skipper' returned to Freer Road distraught by what had happened. Yes, it was a cowardly act carried out by a racist but as they say in boxing "Protect yourself at all times." And if you can't do that, then learn to run.

Most black people turn to religion or music as a means of voicing feelings and dealing with life's stresses. Through religion, music, and song some people find hope and strength but for me it would by learning martial arts. I decided right there to stop trying to fit in because I was born to stand out and just like in my early school days I was willing to fight for my rights.

During my time at Great Barr School the show of black unity served to dispel the threat of attack from the marauding mass of white hooligans who attempted to injure us on a daily basis. Martial arts guaranteed that I possessed individual power and inner strength through learning and I harnessed skills that enabled me to dismiss any such threat for the rest of my life.

PLAYLIST 4

SOUL & REGGAE INSPIRTATIONAL MUSIC

SOUL MUSIC

Aretha Franklin - Young, Gifted And Black
Bobby Womack - Across 110th Street
Brother to Brother - In The Bottle
Charles Mingus - Moanin'
Chet Baker - Almost Blue
Chocolate Milk - Action Speaks Louder Than Words, New World Order, Future Shock, Give Me Your Love (Love Song), Little Child Running Wild, Move On Up, Pusherman, Superfly, People Get Ready, Freddie's Dead (Theme From Superfly)
Darondo - Let My People Go
Don McClain & The Electrifying Cashmeres - Summertime
Don Hathaway - The Ghetto
Earth Wind & Fire - Africano, In The Stone, Shining Star, Fantasy
Edwin Starr - Ain't It Hell Up In Harlem
Etta James - Woman
Sly & The Family Stone - Family Affair
George Benson & Earl Klugh - Jamaica
George Soulé - Get Involved
Ghetto Kitty - Stand Up And Be Counted
Gil Scott Heron - Winter In America, The Revolution Will Not Be Televised
Gil Scott Heron & Brian Jackson - Willing

Isaac Hayes - Theme From Shaft
James Brown - The Boss
Kool And The Gang - Summer Madness
Lack Of Afro Featuring Wayne Gidden - A Time For
Lee Fields And The Sugarman & Co - Stand Up
Leo's Sunshipp - Give Me The Sunshine
Lonnie Liston Smith - Give Peace A Chance
Marvin Gaye - Inner City Blues (Make Me Wanna Holler)
Marvin Gaye - Just like Music, Third World Girl, What's Going On, Where Are We Going?, You're The Man
Maze Featuring Frankie Beverly - We Are One
Melvin Van Peebles - Won't Bleed Me
Mary Clayton - Southern Man
Miles Davis - Blue In Green
Bongi & Nelson - Do You Remember Malcolm
New York City - Sanity
Nina Simone - Aint Got No - I Got Life, Feeling Good, Revolution
Quincy Jones - Everything Must Change, The Dude
Ray Charles - Mother, Say No More
Roy Ayers Ubiquity - Everybody Loves The Sunshine
Roy Ayers & Wayne Henderson - Thank You, Thank You
S.O.U.L - Tell It Like It Is
Sam Cooke - A Change Is Gonna Come, Chain Gang
Sarah Vaughan - Inner City Blues (Make Me Wanna Holler)
Sharon Jones & The Dap Kings - Genuine Pts. 1 & 2
Miles Davis - So What
Sons of Slum - Right On

The Staple Singers - Brand New Day
Harold Melvin & The Blue Notes - Wake Up Everybody
Ray Charles - That Lucky Old Sun
The Jacksons - Show You The Way To Go
The O'Jays - Back Stabbers
The Real Thing - Children Of The Ghetto, Stanhope Street
The Stylistics - People Make The World Go Round
The Undisputed Truth - Smiling Faces Sometimes
War - Slipping Into Darkness, The World Is A Ghetto
Weldon Irvine - Music Is The Key
William De Vaughn - Be Thankful For What You Got
Willie Hutch - Brother's Gonna Work It Out.

REGGAE INSPIRATIONAL

Alton Ellis - Blackman's Word
Alva Lewis - Revelation
Bob & Marcia - Young, Gifted And Black
Bob Andy - Life
Bob Marley & The Wailers - The Oppressed Song
Boris Gardiner - Every Nigger Is A Star
Culture - Innocent Blood
Derrick Harriott - Message From A Black Man
Hugh Mundell - Book Of Life
Jackie Brown - Third World Children
Jimmy Cliff - I'm Free
Keith Poppin - Get Together
Ken Boothe - Is It Because I'm Black?
King Chubby (Junior Byles) - Live As One
Leroy Sibbles - Be A Man

Linton Kwesi Johnson - Reality Poem, Dread Beat An' Blood
Lloyd Parks - We'll Get Over It, Slaving
Marcus Reid - Poor Man Cry
Mutabaruka - Any Which Way Freedom
Pat Kelly - Talk About Love
Senior Soul - Is it Because I'm Black?
The Gaylads - Young Gifted And Black
The Heptones - Book Of Rules
Steel Pulse - Handsworth Revolution
Zap-Pow -This Is Reggae Music

5

THE WONDER YEARS

UK Reality

The popularity of late night blues parties like Hampton Road, 104 Heathfield and St Peter's Road quenched the thirst young people had for music. Black people were still being turned away from clubs in town or, the club DJs did not accept black people and could not cater for black music tastes. There weren't any black music radio stations except for an hour of 'Erskine T' on Sundays. People were hungry and wanted to hear the music, socialise, and experience the 'vibe'. This fuelled the need for promoters, venues, artists, bands, sound systems and DJs alike.

In 1978 Lewis had an eighteenth birthday party that was 'off the hook.' He didn't ask for much as he'd already got a car the year before. He wanted a birthday party and my parents thought this was fitting as their little boy was turning into a wonderful young man. In those days, birthday parties were at home as the option to rent a club was not available. On the day, we went to Black Wax Record Shop on Lozells Road and spent a fortune on the latest music. The big tune of the era was *Natural Woman*, a classic lovers' rock track.

My mum, Aunt Lee and the other women cooked

enough food to feed the multitudes, whilst my dad made safe all the items of furniture that could be moved. By the time we returned from the record shop at around 5pm, the party had already begun. As we walked down Freer Road, we could see people hanging out of their bedroom windows and loads of people standing outside the house. We went straight in and set up our little stereo sound, putting speakers in each room at the highest point which was a cabinet in one room and a wall unit in the other. We wired up the amplifier and deck and sorted out the music we had just purchased and started to play. It's fair to say that most of the black people from Great Barr, Broadway and Holte schools made an appearance at some point throughout the night – the party rocked until the early hours. My parents were legends; how they kept the food and drink going for so long has always been a mystery to me and amazingly, people who had crashed out were still eating in the morning. Lewis's 18th party was the first of what would become a series of legendary parties over the next few years. All brought about because of who my brother had become as a man and bore testament to his great character. I think it was at this point that my brother got a taste for promotions.

My brother and I always went out together. He always knew where the latest places were to go that had a buzz. One day bought tickets for us to watch Bob Marley, live at the Odeon Cinema in Birmingham. However, Bob Marley was not as important to me as playing basketball; I had a match on that day and was not going to let my team down.

He also got tickets for us to see the band Chic, then the 1979 Miss World Contest held in London, where we actually got to meet the third-placed contestant, Miss Jamaica, the beautiful Debbie Campbell. She was totally grounded and I had never before seen such a beautiful woman. At this point I realised that Jamaican women are indeed the finest women in the world.

At the age of 18, my brother had firmly established himself as a socialite. His lifestyle changed and became alien to me. Let me explain – he declined a company car and drove a bigger car to work than his boss, got married at 18, bought a house and went to the gym and spa just to read newspapers. This was an interesting but confusing time for me as I saw my brother maturing into a man before my very eyes. We had always enjoyed similar activities but now his world was expanding far beyond my comprehension.

It's All about Bass

After leaving school, in summer 1979, I ordered a pair of high-quality speaker boxes to be made. A Rasta carpenter called Joey was one of the carpenters in Lion Sound System. He already had empty speaker cabinets waiting for order in his room and he suggested that I buy some speakers and come back to him. That set me off on an exercise to find out which speakers were the best to use.

Danny was my neighbour and a keen electrician who bought magazines every week; his bedroom was full of electronics and sound system information. His school friends were all sound men but unlike them he was a practising Christian and played guitar at church. Danny was always doing electrical work such as fixing amplifiers, turntables and talking about specifications. He told me to invest in Richard Allen speakers and that although the cost was substantial, the sound would be second to none. Naturally, I took his advice and eventually took them to Joey for him to make up into my boxes. There were discussions about which padding to use to maximise the bass output; I wanted speakers that sounded just like the ones in Sydney's room when I first heard Third World's album, *96 Degrees*. When my boxes were ready for collection it was one of the proudest days of my life and my most treasured purchase up to that point.

Jacob Sound System

1980! The beginning of an era, the age of miracles and wonder. Errol and Mikey built a genuine sound system and as we were neighbours, we instantly became members of the crew. The physical sound system was housed at Glen, Bear and Wriggler's flat which was directly opposite our house. Glen, a carpenter by trade, used his carpentry skills to build the speaker units. The sound was called Jacob and all day on most days, loud reggae music with its traditional heavy bass line would be heard playing as they rehearsed.

Hanging out with the crew became a daily activity which gave me the opportunity to get hands-on experience and practice in selecting and playing the tunes on the sound system. I loved delving into the record box and selecting from the thousands of vinyl records that were stored there. I thoroughly enjoyed using the pre-amplifier and experimenting with the knobs to adjust the equalisation and frequency of the records as they played so as to make them more interesting.

Before Jacob, sound systems and how they worked as a business did not interest me. In my mind, all the selector had to do was play records of their choice in no particular order. However, it wasn't long before I realised and understood that being an operator and selector inolved intrinsic skill. The operator constantly tweaked and turned the knob settings to get the maximum effect from the music. For instance, the bass is used to create suspense and release in the music so when the operator wants to create suspense in the music flow, the bass would be reduced or entirely removed. Then to get the crowd going, the bass would be reintroduced.

There were guys in the crew who knew everything about the music they played. That is, where it was made, when it was made, which studio it was recorded at and the studio's history. It was simply mind-blowing but personally, I didn't care where it was made. Whilst knowing that there were different record labels for a reason, I didn't take part in the discussions about the studios that produced the music e.g. Coxsone, Studio One and Treasure Island Records. It became apparent to me that having intimate knowledge about the music enabled the crew to communicate effectively with the partygoers.

It was at this point I started to understand the process of using music as a tool to generate income from alcohol. They needed to keep the crowd entertained which meant that they were able to sell lots of alcohol to keep the business going.

Jacob's jewel in the crown was the infamous 'Daddy Stones' who was a big promotional factor for any sound. 'Daddy Stones' kept the blues rocking until at least lunch time the next day! His skills enabled him always to play the right music at the right time in order to keeping the drinks flowing. His deep, gravelly toned voice would echo on the microphone above the music and he had the ability to read a crowd from the first song. It was as if he had a sixth sense as he always knew what tempo the crowd wanted the music at. He had the ability to 'sing jay' on the music and the blues were always 'nice'.

Raving at blues became a weekly activity and I went to parties to engage with women and not particularly to listen to the music. Any music would do and as long as women were there, I was happy to support the bar.

The Freer Road posse knew all sorts of people and as the blues grew into a local attraction, all sorts of people started to make it their regular Saturday night spot. The posse was extended to include new people from Handsworth who transcended the customer role and became friends and family with us. One of these people is 'Bigga Ford' who we knew as one of the 'Wassifa' sound crew who we knew from school. However, until this period we didn't really have a reason to chill together. The blues party and the desire to rave became the reason.

'Bigga Ford' was a promoter who had a reputation as a martial artist and he was one of Sensei Richards's students. He was a strapping guy of similar build to me, about 6'5" tall, friendly, approachable and had a dark chocolate complexion. Little did I know then that this guy was about to become my second brother.

'Bigga's' name was synonymous with his character and his life style. He was the ultimate 'Raver', promoter, and hustler. He was not a gangster which was quite refreshing for me as it allowed us to become as close as family. He was well networked and knew where the parties of worth were being held each weekend. One night 'Bigga' and I planned to go out raving and since he loved to drink, I was the nominated driver. After picking up 'Bigga' and Rox-roy, aka 'Roxy', we went to collect 'Bigga's' date who brought her friend along with her. That night we all raved at a party in Sheldon, Birmingham.

'Bigga' provided me with a get out of jail card with

girlfriends and whenever we partied I didn't take girlfriends, thus increasing my chances of 'pulling' another woman for the night. That night we left the party in the early hours of the morning, but instead of dropping everyone off at their respective homes, we all ended up crashing at Roxy's flat and it wasn't very long before 'Bigga' disappeared into a separate room with his companion, leaving myself, 'Roxy' and 'Bigga's' girl's friend alone in the living room.

Despite having been with 'the friend' at the party for several hours I hadn't really looked at her. 'Roxy' was busy trying to chat her up and begged her to come into his bedroom but she refused point blank. In his frustration he began to pull on her arm. She strenuously objected to him grabbing her, then sat on the settee next to me and asked me to stop 'Roxy' bothering her. I started to laugh, and looked over my shoulder to see 'Roxy' standing there with his arms outstretched and his mouth wide open as though dumbfounded. I didn't say a word and just gave him the 'get lost look' and continued laughing at him. He came back into the room on several occasions, and at one point he started stamping around, cursing and mumbling under his breath. Eventually he gave in, went to his room and stayed there! After 'Roxy's' episode, 'the girl' and I sat in front of the fire in the living room and talked nonstop until the morning broke. Eventually, 'Bigga' emerged from the room and I dropped the girls back. Finally, I arrived home feeling tired, but content.

The next day, 'the girl' called before coming to

spend the day with me and that was the start of our relationship. She was chilled out and seemed like a well-spoken home girl - we got on really well together. Her parents were also Jamaican and took to me straightaway. She looked after her niece from Wales and always brought her along whenever she visited us in Aston. She appeared to love children and it wasn't long before she was expecting our first child and moved into my flat, which was on Broughton Road, Handsworth. Cutting a long story short we went on to have three sons, young lions, called Nathan, Benjamin RIP, and Aaron Broomfield. All of them have 'Lewis' as a middle name and it is hoped that one day they will ask me "Why?", and then I can tell them all about their Grandpa.

Love & Basketball

By now, both Ivor and I had grown 'dreads' whilst continuing to play cadet-ranked basketball with no undue concerns expressed by anybody. However, this was soon to change. After a training session, we were taken aside and given an ultimatum by the coach of the Birmingham Bullets team. He said if we wanted to be on the team we would have to cut our hair. I stood there shouting out "what has my hair got to do with the game, coach?" The coach maintained his composure and reiterated the instruction and ultimatum. I looked across at Ivor and knew exactly what he was thinking at that very moment. We should have both 'double whammied' him to the ground and walked out of there but we weren't gangster enough, well at least Ivor wasn't. I, on the other hand was fuming; it was as if my insides were on fire. Was I having a déjà vu moment from Great Barr School here? Instinctively, I wanted to start fighting. Here I was, along with Ivor, having just sacrificed what promised to be a good sporting career and the achievement of something special with a group of guys.

Basketball continued to be a part of my staple diet and although the prospect of a career in sport appeared to be on hold, my yearning for playing the game did not wane. Basketball had changed; gone were the Converse All Stars generation and in came the era of 'Air Time'. There was a whole new attitude to the game and basketball was alive in the city.

It seemed logical for me to start a basketball team, which I did. The team was called the Assassins and we were in the West Midland Basketball League. I wanted to create a team reminiscent of the Harlem Globetrotters; a team that could play, entertain and win convincingly. There was a plethora of former national league players available to choose from over the summer months. However, most of my former England buddies, including my sidekick Ivor, along with Wisdom, Nehemiah, Cheese, and Smithy combined to make the nucleus of the team. But the 'piece de resistance' was recruiting an extremely skilled player called Patrick who lived in Small Heath. Patrick was 6' 4", and had an upright posture with the look of a real Harlem Globetrotter. He had a slightly conical shaped head and a wide, full-lipped mouth with gleaming white teeth that were permanently on display – because he was either smiling or scowling. His arms seemed to reach the floor and he had really large hands. Patrick was a lean, mean, 'dunkin' machine and had the ability to elevate himself above 11ft with the utmost grace and finesse. His deadly-three point shot that rarely missed the hoop and together with his dribbling skills he was a formidable force to be reckoned with. However, he was also a very angry person on the court and his lack of discipline and resulting behaviour prevented him from furthering his career in the game. But he was perfect for the team.

The league had several impressive and established clubs but we swept them aside and quickly became an unstoppable force in the West Midlands. It wasn't long before referees started trying to cheat us out of games to reduce the embarrassing score lines. The Assassin Basketball Club trained and had matches at Broadway School that had enabled me to meet the resident Youth Worker there called Judah, who ran an out-of-school youth club at Broadway. He was a long-time rasta with thick matted binds and a very charismatic personality. He was always friendly and positive towards the youths. Judah was much older than me but we quickly became friends. He encouraged me to do a few sessions at his youth club which then became regular work for me and in time Ivor also got a job there. Things moved on and a new youth worker started at Broadway, named

Keith Reid. Keith was equally enthusiastic about working with young people and was a passionate football player.

After the adventure with the Assassins that year we decided to merge with a team called Oaklands whose base was at Holyhead School in Handsworth. That team had a long history and already had several imposing players turning out to battle each week. Oaklands was a youth centre that organised an annual sports tournament. The Handsworth Sports Day was a multi-sport tournament which involved clubs from around the country. Aside from the league activities, this was the biggest game in the calendar each year. The sports, namely basketball, netball and football, took place at various school campuses and following a gruelling day of tournaments, an awards ceremony and after-party took place.

Weekends were packed with sporting activities and Sundays officially became a routine sport activity day which was used to recover from raving the night before. Normally after reaching home at 7am, I would freshen up and grab my kit bag from the boot of my car and arrive for training at Dojos Gym before 9am, to do a two-hour aerobic workout with 'Captain Boogie', 'Eastman' and a few others.

The class was always packed with enthusiastic women and the 'Captain' played the latest club grooves to suit the mood of the ladies. Following aerobics I would take a two-hour intensive karate class normally comprising of sparring and mastering fighting techniques. Then my next stop, at 2pm, was basketball at Holyhead School. Another sport was roller-skating at Handsworth Park and again the 'Captain' was the organiser, promoter and DJ, providing the perfect evening's entertainment for the masses. After about three hours of rolling, rocking, jumping and skanking we would eventually leave the skate rink. After the hustle of the day, there was one thing written in stone – going home to my mum's, for my Sunday dinner.

Party after Rollerskating

This party, in Ladywood, was guaranteed to be rocking and in addition to the day's sports, another hour was spent in my bedroom, pumping iron and working on my biceps to prepare for the party that night. Having arrived at around midnight, the party was already packed. I edged my way into the main room and found a spot to build a spliff in peace, and then went outside to get some fresh air, with my drink in one hand and spliff in the other. Several people were outside on the balcony talking, drinking and chilling in the warm evening breeze.

Then I suddenly realised that the horizontal brickwork on the wall was now running vertically!! My head was down on the floor. Looking up I saw the guys standing over me, their mouths wide open in shock. Having seen me drop like a stone they literally froze. I clambered to my feet, dazed, confused and totally embarrassed when Eton shouted "HULK!" What just happened?" and then burst into laughter which gave everyone the green light to do the same. It must have been funny to see 'Hulk', the big man drop down flat on his face in public. Thankfully, no serious injuries were sustained, just a deflated ego and major personal embarrassment. Eton told everybody the story and everyone had a good laugh that night – at my expense.

The Beachwear House Party

By the age of 20 my brother had achieved so much and people loved him. He was upwardly mobile as were most of his associates. He got on with everybody including all the rough necks in my squad and the ladies loved him even though he was married.

Alongside his day job as a surveyor, he became quite a promoter by night. His old job at the Night Out in Birmingham had given him a taste for the celebrity lifestyle. He mixed with the 'middle class yuppies' and was part of 'the wine bar crew' who drove fancy cars.

He had the brilliant idea of hosting a beachwear party at his house. I was in charge of security and I ensured no one entered the party unless they wore beach or swimwear. The men pulled up in their cars thinking they could get past me without the appropriate attire. However, they instantly went home to get their trunks after seeing the most beautiful girls turning out en mass. The ladies dropped their coats from their shoulders, and the doors literally opened. Groups of guys wearing trunks stood with their mouths wide open as girl after girl came into the party. The neighbours stood outside their houses and smiled as they watched the parade of swimsuit-clad women arriving as if for a gala ball event. Mr Merry and Coptic Crew sound played at the party all night, blasting out rare groove tunes. Wow what a night!

Keith Copeland 'the mouth of Aston' from Freer Road was there and as they say never judge a book by its cover. It's amazing how humble the mighty can become when they choose to mature. The only time Keith was ever humbled was when his dad was cussing him, he always showed the respect due to his dad. I thought Keith being at the party was a recipe for disaster. Naturally, he was going to have a good time but not only did he actually behave himself and not get too loud and crazy, he actually revealed a side of himself that had not been seen before. Keith was a quite pleasant and charming man when he wanted to be. Forever the showman of course, but he was the life of the party. There wasn't a big tune played where you wouldn't hear his booming voice above the music, shouting out, "pull up" to the selector. He was in his element dancing with all the naked girls.

My sister was being harassed by a man. This angered Keith who went crazy and threw the guy out of the party threatening to decapitate him if he even thought about coming back. He was really protective of her because she was our sister. He earned my respect that night and my view of him changed forever. It was a welcome change for me not to have played the 'heavy' as I would have behaved in exactly the same way and if Keith hadn't thrown him out, I would have!! Nuff respect Keith RIP.

In 1977, my brother got a burgundy Morris Marina off my Dad when he passed his driving test. So in March 1979 I was equally keen to pass my driving test and I had already been driving for years, albeit illegally, with no problems. However, I booked a few driving lessons with Garnett driving school just to be on the safe side. I passed my test the first time and the very same night I drove Peter's car to the Pink Coconut in Derby, with the crew. Peter asked me to drive his car and 'Eastman' drove his silver grey Ford Capri. On the way back my car seemed to be dragging somewhat and there was a distinct aroma of burning rubber - I had driven all the way back with the car's hand brake still firmly on. The 'free loaders' laughed me down for it.

Those were the wonder years, a time of awe and questions, a time of new beginnings, friendships, optimism, and joy. This era was filled with so many positive memories of things that happened to excite us in our lives as teenagers; when our lives and futures were full of endless possibilities.

'Memories are strange things. There are tangible memories that can be proven factually, suppressed memories that are clouded recollections of actual

events, memories that are a mixture of real and unreal events, and there are memories based on imagination.'

PLAYLIST 5

LOVERS' ROCK & 'ROOTSY LOVERS' MUSIC

LOVERS' ROCK

15-16-17 - Girls Imagination
Administrators - Emergency, She's My Lady
Aswad - I Need Your Love
Barry Biggs - Love You Baby, Sideshow, Wide Awake In A Dream
Beshara - Men Cry Too
Bunny Maloney - Baby I've Been Missing You, Lady Of Magic
Carlton & His Shoes - Mood For Love
Carroll Thompson - Hopelessly In Love, I'm So Sorry
Chosen Few - Love Between A Boy And Girl
Dawn Penn - You Don't Love Me (No, No, No)
Deborah Glasgow - Give Me That Touch, This Love, Knight In Shining Armour
Dee Sharp - Let's Dub It Up
Derrick Lara - Come On Over
Donna Rhoden - Be Kind To My Man, It's True
Eargasm - This Is Lovers Rock
Fredrica Tibbs - Undying Love
Heptics - Natural Woman
Hortense Ellis - Unexpected Places
In Crowd - Getting Cozy
In Crowd Featuring Jah Stitch - Baby My Love
Intense - Mellow
Intense - On My Mind, You Are The One

Investigators - Baby I'm Yours, Woman I Need Your Loving, Living In A World Of Magic, Love Is What You Make It

Janet Kay - Rock The Rhythm, Silly Games, I Do Love You

Jean Adebambo - I've Made Up My Mind, Paradise

John Holt - A House Is Not A Home

John McLean - Truly Bowled Over, If I Gave My Heart To You

Junior English - In Loving You, Never Lose Never Win

Keith Douglas - Cool Down Amina

Kofi - Black Pride, Didn't I, Looking Over Love

Leo Hall - Let's Dub It Up

Leroy Simmonds - At The Dance

Lloyd Parks - Reservation For Two

Louisa Mark - Sixth Street, Keep It Like It Is, Caught You In A Lie, Even Though You're Gone

Love & Unity And Ranking Bogart - Put It On

Love Joys - Sweet Feelings

Love Structure - Doorway Of Love

Marie Pierre - Walk Away, Can't Go Through (With Life)

Matumbi - After Tonight, The Man In Me, Point Of View (Squeeze A Little Lovin')

Motion - No Man Is An Island

Natural Ites - Lately

Pablo Moses - Dubbing Is A Must

Paulette Tajah - 'Cos You Love Me Baby, I Don't Wanna Lose You Now

Revelation - Why Do You Cry?, With You Boy

Riot Squad - I Would Like To Love You

Roland Burrell - Stormy Night
Ruddy Thomas - Key To The World, Nice And Easy
Ruddy Thomas & Susan Cadogan - (You Know How To Make Me) Feel So Good

'ROOTSY LOVERS'

Aaron Black - Hang On
African Brothers - Gimme Gimme African Love
African Youth - Forward Down A Channel One
Al Campbell - Try My love, When The Grass Is Green
Andell Forgie - Don't Underpay Us
Anthony Johnson - Telling My Friends About You, We Na Give Up
B.B. Seaton - Proud As I Am, I'm Trying
Barry Biggs - Work All Day
Barry Brown - Big Big Pollution, Give Love, Give Me Your Love, If I Give My love, Let's Unite, Make It With You, Tourist Season, We Just Can't Live Like This, Ketch- A-Fire, Party Night aka Let's Go To The Blues
Big Youth - Double Attack, Hit The Road Jack, It's Not Unusual
Bim Sherman - Golden Locks
Bob Andy - Going Home, Unchained
Bobby Melody - Get Up And Dance
Boris Gardiner - You Make Me Feel Brand New
Bunny Lie Lie - Something Going To Happen
Carlton And The Shoes - Sweet Feeling
Christine - Saturday Night
Bushman - Creatures of the Night
Carl Meeks - Tuff Scout

Dave Robinson - Native Woman
Dean Frazer, Sly Dunbar & Clive Hunt - Out On Bail
Delroy Denton & The Silvertones - Sufferer's Choice
Delroy Williams - Babylon Boy, Ten To One, This Love, I Stand Black, My Cecilia, Tune in
Dennis Brown - Ain't That Loving You, Black Magic Woman, Coming Home Tonight, Gimme Your Loving, Here I Come, How Can I Leave You, Lately Girl, Let Me Love You, Little Green Apples, Money In My Pocket, Musical Heatwave, Perhaps, Queen Majesty, Rain Drops Keep Falling, Rocking Time, Rolling Down, Running Around, Love Light, Natural Mystic, Satisfaction Feeling, Sitting And Watching, Some Like It Hot, Someone Special, Summertime, Drifter, No Man Is An Island, Deceiving Girl
Dennis Brown/Sly & Robbie - Sitting & Watching
Dennis Walks - Drifter
Derrick Harriott -Tonight, Tonight, I'm Your Puppet
7th Extension/Ranking Devon - Hard Time/All Nation Have To Bow
Devon Russell & The Yoruba Singers - Roots Natty Roots
Don Carlos - Favorite Cup, Feeling Of Love, Fight Fight, Gimme Gimme Your Love, I Love Jah, Johnny Big Mouth, Just A Passing Glance, Nice Time (Late Night Blues), Money And Women, Prophecy, Roots Man Party, Satta Massa Gana, Untrue Girl, White Squall, Spread Out, In Pieces, At The Bus Stop, I'm Leaving, Mr Sun, Oh Girl, Crazy Girl, Jamaican Woman
Don Carlos & Captain Sinbad - I'm Not Crazy
Don Carlos Featuring Christos DC - Righteous Chant

Dona V. - Lady Pullover
Earl Cunningham - Cool Profile, The Words Of The Father, Jail House
Earl Sixteen - My Number One
Earl Sixteen & The Heptones - The World Has Begun
Echo Minott - Rip & Run Off
Eek A Mouse - Do You Remember
Dennis Brown - Emmanuel God Is With Us
Errol Dunkley - A Little Way Different, My Baby Is Gone, Put Down the Gun aka Stop The Gun Shooting
Errol Gordon - Message
F Stewart - Do Good
Fabian - Prophecy
Freddie McGregor - Homeward Bound, Loving Pauper, Holy Mount Zion, Big Ship, Chant It Down, Leave Yah, I Man A Rasta, I'm A Revolutionist, Jah Help The People, Joggin', Just Don't Want To Be Lonely, Look Like Me, Love One Another, Mr Officer, Little Girl A Nuh Time Fe Skin Up, Natural Collie/Natural Dub, Not As Happy, Rastaman Camp, Rhythm So Nice, Sweet Lady, That Girl (Groovy Situation), To Be Poor Is A Crime, We Need More Love, Let Him Try, Never Get Away, Prophecy
General Echo - Arleen
Gregory Isaacs - Mr Cop
Gregory Isaacs - Promised Land
Guardian Angel - China Gate
Heptones - Cool Rasta
Hopeton Lewis - Grooving Out On Life
Horace Andy - Money Money, Problems, Ain't No Sunshine, Angel Call Woman, Cuss Cuss, Don't Say

No, Don't Try To Use Me, Girl I Love You, Just Say Who,
Let's Live In Love, Lonely Woman, Them Never Tell I,
Nice And Easy, Respiration, Rock To Sleep, Show And
Tell, Tell Me Why, This World, You Are My Angel

Horace Andy & Tappa Zukie - Natty Dread A Weh
She Want

Hortense Ellis - I'm Just A Girl

Hue B - Everyday Thing

Hugh Griffiths - Splendid Things, This Little Heart Of
Mine

Hugh Mundell - Can't Pop No Style, Feeling Alright Girl,
Jacqueline, Your Face Is Familiar

I Kong - The Way It Is

I Roy - Don't Get Weary Joe Frazier

I Roy - Welding

In Crowd - Back A Yard, His Majesty Is Coming, Born
In Ethiopia

Inner Circle - Natty Dread, We 'A' Rockers

Jackie Edwards - Sexy Sandy, Clock On The Wall, I
Want A Love I Can See

Jackie Paris - Sinner Man

Jacob Miller - Baby I Love You So, Let Me Love You, All
Night 'Till Daylight, Too Much Imitator, Mrs. Brown

Jacob Miller & Inner Circle - I've Got The Handle, Suzy
Wong

Jimmy London - I'm Your Puppet, Till I Kiss You

Jimmy Riley - Delicious, Love And Devotion, Think
Before You Talk

Joe Higgs - More Slavery

Johnny Clarke - Left With A Broken Heart

John Holt - In The Corner, Love I Can Feel, Police In

Helicopter, Walk Away, You'll Never Find Another Love Like Mine, Ghetto Girl

Johnny Clarke - Baby Don't Go, Bad Days Are Going Away, Dance To The Music, Everyday Wondering, Lift Yourself Up, Morning Star, Ride On Girl, Rocking To The A-Class Champion, Stranger In Love, Ten To One, Wante Wante Can't Get It, You Better Try, Love Me Forever, Live Up Jah Man, Can't Get Enough

Johnny Osbourne & the Viceroys- Sing Jay Style, Johnny Osbourne - Love Is Here To Stay, Rock With You

Junior Brown - What A Disaster

Junior Byles And Rupert Reid - Remember Me

Junior Byles - Curly Locks, Fade Away

Junior Delgado - Famine, Trickster, Hypocrites, Speak Softly Love

Junior Hibbert - Really For A Reason

Junior Murvin - Bad Man Posse, Muggers In The Street, Police And Thieves, Cool Out Son, False Teaching

Junior Reid - Know Myself

Junior Roots - Natty Dread Time

Junior Tucker - 16 (Into The Night)

Justin Hinds - Love In The Morning, Carry Go Bring Come

Keeling Beckford - One A Way Man

Keith & Tex - Stop That Train

Keith Hudson - True To My Heart

Keith Rowe - Groovy Situation

Ken Boothe - Down By The River

King Everald - Life Can Be Funny

Lacksley Castell - Just Too Young

Lacksley Castell – You Over There
Leroy Brown & The Black Traps – Blood A Go Run
Leroy Roots – Shocking
Leroy Sibbles – Love And Happiness, Love In The Morning, Lying Girl
Leroy Smart – Mr. Smart
Leroy Smart – I've Got Love
Sugar Minott – Is it True
Linval Thompson – Baby Father, Cool Down Your Temper, Danger In Your Eyes, Don't Give Up, If I Follow My Heart, Mr Boss Man, Natty Dread Girl, Sukumaka
Linval Thompson & Ranking Trevor – Six Babylon
Lion Youth – Chant In A Dance
Little John & Billy Boyo – What You Want To Be, Janet Sinclair
Lloyd Parks – We'll Get Over It
Martin Campbell – Loser
Love Joys – Long lost Lover
Maddo – Little Young Girl
Major Christie – Mama Struggle
Marcia Aitken – I'm Still In Love
Marcia Griffiths – Hurting Inside, Children Of Israel, Dreamland, Peaceful Woman, Untrue Love
Matumbi – Pretender
Max Romeo – Where Is The Love
Max Romeo & The Upsetters – One Step Forward
The Maytones – Who Feel It
Michael Palmer – Come Natural
Michael Prophet – I Want Your Heart, Love And Unity, Sweet Loving, Woman I Love, Serious Reasoning, Fight To The Top, Let It Rain, Trouble Me

Michael Prophet & Scientist - You Are No Good
Milton Bull - My Baby Is Gone
More Relation - Misled Love
Dennis Brown - Moving Away
Tappa Zukie - Dub MPLA
Mr. Lonely Man - Sometimes
Otis Gayle - What You Won't Do For Love
Owen Gray - Ballistic Affair
Pablo Moses - A Song, Music Is My Desire
Pat Kelly - Summer Time, One Man Stand
Pat Kelly & Ranking Trevor - It's A Good Day
Patrick Andy - Black Girl, Clarendon Girl
Paula Clarke - Skip And Dance
Pete Campbell - Does She Have A Friend For Me
Peter Tosh - Brand New Second Hand
Phillip Fraser - When I Run Out, Girl You Hold Me, I
Who Have Nothing, Never Let Go, Reggae Explosion,
Tonight, You Will Be Sorry
Barry Brown - Politician
Prince Far I - Blessed Is The Man
Prince Fatty Featuring Winston Francis & Horseman
- Come On Girl
Prince Lincoln & The Royal Rasses - Unconventional
People, Humanity, Dreadlocks Man
Prince Lincoln Thompson & Royal Rasses - Revelation
Prince Lincoln - Old Time Friends
Prince Far I Featuring Ashantie Roy - Throw Away
Your Gun
Private Tabby - If You Leave Me
Roland Burrell - Stormy Night
Roman Stewart & Dave Barker - Changing Times

Ronnie Davis - Strange Things
Roy Rankin & Raymond Naptali - Go Deh In A Late Night Blues
Sam Cooke - Teenage Sonata
Sammy Dread - African Girl
Sammy Dread & Papa Tullo - Morning Love
Sheila Hylton - The Bed's Too Big Without You
Shy FX Featuring Liam Baily - Soon Come
Sophia George - Real International
The Invaders - Soulful Music
Still Cool - What A Shame
Storm - Sitting In The Bush
Sugar Black - Yesterday Once More
Sugar Minott - Something Wrong
Tappa Zukie - She Want A Phensic, What Da Do
Terence Smith & Cassette & Tape - V.I.B.
The Dynamic Four - Let's Make Love
The Dynamics - Bring Me Up
The Heptones Featuring Joe White - Give Me The Right
The Blackstones - Fighting To The Top, Tribute To Studio One
The Chantells - Man In Love
The Mighty Diamonds - Tell Me What's Wrong
The Maytones - Money Worries
The Meditations - Miracles, No More Friends, No Peace
The Mighty Diamonds - Country Living
The Never Ending Wailers - I'm Still Waiting
The Rolands Featuring U Brown - Nobody Cares
The Royals - Pick Up The Pieces

The Silvertones - Smile
T Brothers - She Loves You
The Tamlins - Hurting Me, Baltimore
The Uniques - Queen Majesty
The Uprising Maytone - Unchangeable Love
Tony Brevett - Don't Get Weary
Tony Lowe - Line Stepper
Tony Washington - Tribute To Muhammad Ali
Trevor Byfield - Jah Guide
Trinity - Three Piece Suit
Tristan Palmer - Bad Minded, Ghetto King, Girl I Love,
Miserable Woman, Collie Man, Joker Lover, Lover Man,
She Only Love Me For My Money, Sit A Wonder
Vin Gordon - Grass In The Sun
Lloyd Jones - Daydreaming Of Africa
Wayne Wade - Black Is Our Colour, I Kissed A Rose,
Run Come Rally, Man Of The Living
Billy Boyo - Wicked She Wicked
Willie Williams - I Am A Winner, No One Can Stop Us
Winston Hussey - A Tear Drops

6

MUSIC, POWER &
A NEW NAME - RASTAFARI

Woodstock in my Garden

In 1975 Britain's streets were tough and racist graffiti was a constant reminder of life in the poorest areas. It is fair to say that blacks were still somewhat segregated from the rest of British society and for the children of the Jamaican migrants, life on the street was brutal.

The summer of 1976 is officially the best summer on record and will forever dominate the memories of those who were lucky enough to have been around then. This was a time when there seemed to be endless days of sun and heat and is the time when a whole new world unfolded in front of my eyes. It was the summer of love, a time when a new music just seemed to explode into our consciousness. For the kids born here there was a new swagger about being black British. There was a new British sound called lovers' rock and everyone loved it. Soul music was being remixed into lovers' rock and going down a storm in the party and clubs. Big tunes like Marvin Gaye's *Wake Up Every Body* were covered by reggae artists like Big Youth. I had heard the Marvin Gaye version on the radio but somehow the reggae version was on point and the heavy drum and bass guaranteed to hit the spot.

"One good thing about music is that when it hits you, you feel no pain" **Bob Marley**

There was another festival taking place in Handsworth Park. My brother and I knew about the event but it was on a Sunday and church always takes precedence plus the fact that we were focused on the upcoming annual convention at church.

As Gil Scott Heron has predicted *"The revolution will not be televised"*

One hot sun kissed Sunday afternoon when the world should have been at rest, Handsworth Park (Queen Victoria Park) was alive with the sound of a sweet revolution. There was a strange mystical vibration in the air that day, the gathering of Jah's children for the rapture. The sweet vibration from the bass and the sound of angelic horns and harmonies travelled out into all the land, carried by the wind. It was the Rasta call to prayer on the afternoon breeze. The complex and rhythmical sound of the African drums filled the air and created a cosmic vibration that reached the hearts of Jah's people and beckoned the children to come unto him.

Black people were drawn towards the source of the call and to go out to the meeting place. That day Reggae music filled the airwaves all across the land.

My brother, 'Blackeye', Danny, Boris and I all decided to get out of church and go to the park to see what was going on. We could hear the music calling us from the church, the church people were calling it the 'devil's music' but when that 'devil music' is calling at your soul, then that's when the wheat and the chaff have to separate. We wanted to see what was happening but it wasn't going to be easy. If anyone ever tried to leave the service, one of the numerous church deacons would appear in front of you.

Eventually some of us broke out and as soon as we turned the corner by the church steps we switched into stealth mode and got up to tracking speed, swiftly jogging towards the park. At that point we assumed we would be coming back before service was over and before anyone missed us. As so many people from church lived on Holly Road, we decided to go via the Hamstead Road entrance and tracked up the hill towards the bridge. Plenty of people were heading towards the source of the sound; that mystical sound. When we got over the hill, I couldn't believe my eyes. It felt was as though I had been lifted from this place and taken to another because I had never seen so many Rastas in one place. It seemed as if every single Rasta in the whole world were all in one spot for one reason. This was just how I imagined it would be with my people outside Zion's gates.

My little posse and I meandered around on the periphery of the crowd; I think we stood out a bit and were easily distinguishable from the majority of the revellers as we were the ones dressed up for church with suits and ties on. Everybody else seemed to be adorned in the colourful and majestic regalia of Rastafari, Marcus Garvey and Africa. There were all kinds of dreads and clearly many people had been Rastas for years as their dreads were almost on the ground.

It his was the first time I saw the reggae giants Aswad live and it was the best show that I recall them doing in Birmingham. When the band came on stage, and started playing their song 'Back to Africa', the whole place broke down. That day left a lasting impression in my heart. The music made Africa sound like it was heaven, a place with no fussing and fighting, just everyone uniting. The people were in harmony and a natural mystique was moving through the air. It was my first experience of what belonging to a people really meant. Not because I knew them or associated with them, it was because there was no doubt in my heart that out spirit was the same.

Cultural Awakening

After that particular day in Handsworth Park, there seemed to be an explosion of Rastafarian music, beautiful colours and a higher consciousness which seemed to happen almost overnight. People started to wear clothing embellished with the Red, Gold and Green symbolism, scarves, hats, shoes, flags, pictures, paintings, clocks, carvings and musical instruments. Just about everything that could be customised became stamped with the Rastafarian or Pan African branding. There was a shop just on the corner of Crompton and Heathfield Road, a Rasta Shop selling all kind of African odds and ends known as the Culture Shop. It became a central point for young people who had just left home and got their first housing association flat and needed some African-looking decor for their flat. The shop always had Jamaican and African literature, pictures, paintings, drums, carvings, clothing and accessories on display. The proprietors were a Ras named Shorts and his Queen. The explosion in reggae music made UK-born children aware of the greater plight of black people all over the world and they became more conscious about self, history and religion.

Reggae Music & Sound Awareness

Visiting David and Sydney's home would usually result in us going into their big brother's attic room where we chilled out and listened to their fabulous music collection of vinyl albums and singles. David pulled out the Third World album, *96 Degrees*, and as soon as the needle hit the vinyl, it was clear that this album was something special. This music sounded like the music of angels. It was class, a brand new sound and a move away from the more popular reggae music. This would have a profound impact on how I wanted to listen to music for the rest of my life. A great speaker system is an absolute requirement in order to hear music properly and Sydney's speakers were exceptional.

The Original Rastaman

But where did Rastafari come from and how did it spread amongst the young people? It wasn't taught in schools or churches and whilst there are some references in the vinyl records that may signpost the astute towards the name of Rasta, how did so many people come to accept something so intangible?

By the Eighties things were changing on Freer Road, new people moved into the now refurbished flats which were once family houses. A couple of new faces moved in across the road, one called Hugh Flash and his brother David. They were very distinctive in appearance and in behaviour and I got to know them pretty well. They were real Rastas and they even spoke like Rastas. Hugh was the older of the two, more vocal and he had the softest voice which made him great for reasoning with as he didn't raise his voice. It was more of a discussion than the usual shout down. Suddenly, all my knowledge and beliefs were being dismantled and Rasta truths about our plight and the worship of a white god dawned on me for the first time. I needed more information.

Hugh told me about the honourable Marcus Garvey 'The black Moses' and that he was the most flamboyant among the negroes in Harlem and rode down Manhattan Avenue with 200,000 followers behind him. In 1924 another Jamaican, Leonard Howell, was in Harlem with Marcus Garvey and met up with the Harlem Black Prophets who are the fore-runners of the Rastafarians. His Majesty, Emperor Hailie Selassie was crowned in Ethiopia. He believed HIM (His Imperial Majesty) was the almighty one, Christ reincarnate and the black messiah. He didn't bring a doctrine or religion to Jamaica he just told people the truth about events unfolding in Africa. Thus he is the first Rasta and messenger of the faith. Leonard Howell declared that God is black and renounced King George of England and told people not to pay taxes to the Jamaican government or to King George. The establishment interpreted it to mean insurrection and he was charged with treason and locked up. He eventually returned to St Thomas and created an Ashram called Pinnacle.

Language

The most well-known 'I' phrase within Rastafari culture is InI, ("I-an-I"), which is a collective 'we'. Hugh would say *"I an I, are descendants from Africa but Rasta come to reveal things to the nation to free us from the shackles and chains that 'I an I' were bound in"*. When he spoke about music he said. *"The playing of the drum reaches the heart to a depth more than any other and we respond because all black man was born to play drum because drums is from Africa.*

Drums are used to educate the nation. You can find the real roots if you penetrate the hills of Jamaica."

He continued *"Babylonian uses food as a spiritual warfare against the most high but unfortunately not all who say they are Rastas, are true Rastas. We really have to be careful of what Rasta man partakes in this Babylon and must learn to stay away from their wine of violence, like the Rum and the Hennessey. Their wines and drugs are designed with the wickedest intention and is an enemy to Rastafari and to mankind. Really any man who partakes from the wine of violence is far from the teaching of his majesty. Real Rasta men don't even smoke 'weed' as they don't want to consume fire but instead see the herb as the healing of the nation and not the burning of the nation."*

The key thing with Hugh was he was a real Jamaican Rastaman and talked about his own life in Jamaica. This was not hearsay or holiday experiences nor was it the ranting of 'poppy show' (fake) Rastas, who Hugh said are *"Wolves in sheep clothing who a give 'Natty Dread' a bad name."* Hugh knew everything about Rastas.

Handsworth Revolution

Steel Pulse were Birmingham's offering of a roots group. They were much older than us and had risen almost all the way into the charts without me actually knowing of their existence. The sensational *Handsworth Revolution* album captured the essence of the general feelings amongst black inner city youths here in the UK, so the music caught on and stuck. The 'one dread' look was totally unique amongst the dreads of the day. Most opted for an easier life and parting the dreadlocked 'bind' long before they became thick, or at least as thick as David's binds.

There were lots of opportunities to watch experts first hand. Birmingham was alive and thriving with gigs and shows from all the reggae greats and was considered to be the Jamaica capital of England. The gigs were primarily at black venues such as The Hummingbird and Regal Cinema, Handsworth. Tradition, Louisa Marks, and Carol Thompson were the lovers' rock artists who performed regularly at the Rialto Club on Soho Road. If a lovers' rock artist did not perform at Rialto then they were not credible.

As we became older and bolder we started to venture to larger shows to watch the more hard-core artists like the legendary John Holt at Symphony Hall complete with an orchestra and then again at the Mohammad Ali Centre in Hockley, where the show was totally different and tailored to meet the taste of a more hard-core black audience.

There were Rasta bands by the score and probably the most memorable of them was Culture at Regal Soho Road Handsworth, also Peter Tosh, Third World, Gregory Isaacs, Black Slate, Prince Lincoln and the Royal Rass and many more artists mainly performing at the Hummingbird Club in

Birmingham. Other Jamaican acts included Fred Locks, Inner Circle, Burning Spear, Dennis Brown, Freddy McGregor, Johnny Osborne and even Big Youth. There were also shows at the Porche Club with artists like Sanchez D, Garnet Silk and many others.

LIFE & A PRO BAND

Living in the Ghetto Ain't Easy

In 1980 the Conservative government cared little about black people. The police were complicit in crime, not detecting it or preventing it. They preferred to utilise SUS laws to intimidate young people on the streets whilst they were deeply in cahoots with the main players, in the gangland hierarchies. The police allowed drug dealers to openly sell and distribute drugs openly in black communities.

Fortunately, I got an engineering apprenticeship with an Engineering Company called Wickman Scrivener based in Aston. Some of the others guys were not so successful and left school jobless, forced to sign on as unemployed for a period of time. For some people, this was their sole source of income and they would apportion their fortnightly Giro payment to cover their living costs to the penny. Let's face it, Broadway School was not renowned at the time for producing potential graduates. Certainly, a large group of the boys from the years above me were incarcerated for a variety of activities. Those without work signed on at the dole office on Beacon Hill/Grange Road.

By 1981, things were set to kick off across the

country. A drug-dealer's skirmish with the police escalated and became known as the Handsworth Riots. Night Spot, where I previously worked, was a massive drug shop and where for years 'weed' was openly displayed and sold to the public whilst the police turned a blind eye. The riots started with an attempt to arrest one of the local dealers in the pub at Villa Cross. However, onlookers felt the police were brutalising him whilst restraining him. News of this reached Night Spot and, as they say, the rest is history. Few photographs were taken during the riots because anybody who openly took photographs would be considered an informer. Culturally, this was the norm and the same thing applied to anyone who had a camera at a dance or blues.

My view is that the disturbance created opportunities for the more entrepreneurial amongst the drug crews operating in Night Spot to rob the jewellery shops along the Lozells Road. The escalating disturbance soon affected households along both Lozells and Hunters Roads as well as Barker Street - two other main drug dealing 'hot-spots' in that zone. Word of the upheaval and excitement spread through the community like wild fire and people came out to watch and got caught up in the swaying crowds and useless attempts by the police to stem the unrest. But in the midst of the rushing crowds and charging police, the jewellery shops were all looted and some even burnt down. Now I am not going claim this as a truth but think about it for a moment. For some shop owners it must have been a godsend as many were equally as opportunistic as the many looters and bandits.

According to the manager, getting loans from a local drug dealer was a necessary evil to ensure that we were able to afford to get to gigs. Even now I am not exactly sure why we were penniless after several paid gigs.

After the riots, one of our 'investors' approached the manager asking for a statement to use as an alibi which would place him, at the time of certain activities in the middle of the riot, with us during our rehearsal. It seemed that they had been pulled and needed an alibi. The manager refused to provide the drug man with an alibi for his whereabouts and naturally there was a lot of tension. The drugs man was livid and sought retribution. The money disputes didn't concern the musicians as the drug man did not lend any money to us, but rather to the manager himself and it was the manager he wanted the alibi from.

The Dream

These were the days when everyone in the band had to make decisions about their level of commitment and what we were about to embark on. Personally, this involved me asking my parents to be guarantors for me to purchase a Hand 'HH' PA amplifier and a Fender Rhodes electric piano. My wages from my part-time job at Bill the Bandit were used to purchase the equipment.

Music always played second fiddle to my sports commitments but it was already clear to me that the pendulum had begun to swing towards favouring music and partying over the rigour of the sports life. During this period of my music career, my music began to take on a new meaning. In contrast to the duplicators and the replicators, I was able to create music.

We were writing and composing original music, songs like, *Forget me Not, Culture Dem, Dem A Guh Burn, Destiny, It Takes a Righteous Man, I See HIM* and *Tek A Good Look* which were born out of the Fender Rhodes sound and the influence of Black Uhuru. We soon developed an entourage and 'Big John Haines' came to work for us and I was relieved of driving duties. Valo became our regular van driver, whilst the yard man, Mikey, became our sound engineer. Mikey was also a budding musician and relished the opportunity to make music so he came along to our rehearsals. There was also the infamous 'Buck-I' who moved to live in the Gambia, West Africa, back in the 1980s.

InI Rastafari

Becoming a Rasta was inevitable and some of the members of the band had already started the process. Dreading up served to complete our desired image and I tried to adopt a religious rationale to justify my becoming a Rasta as many of the brethren at Gibson Road church would have agonised over my decision to locks up. Having been baptised a Christian, who was now going to assert that Jesus 'the Christ' had been reincarnated into the personality of Rastafari Emperor Hailie Selassie of Ethiopia? It was imperative for me to find all the religious justification to support such an idea.

To start off the dreading up process, I had to wash my hair, leave it and refrain from combing it. Regularly washing my hair ensured that it became more entangled, and it wasn't too long before my hair began to bind up into individual chunks. This made wearing a hat compulsory at all times, but it wasn't long before my parents realised that their son was now dreading up. My dad was angry but there wasn't a lot he could do about it now. Over the course of a few months, visible individual dreadlocks were now on display. It never really affected my parents as I always wore my hat whilst in their presence. My mum was not at all pleased but instead of complaining she insisted that I come home weekly to have my hair washed by her so that no one could tell her that her son's head was 'dutty'. For a lot of guys with dreads, the prospect of someone washing your hair for you was a dream.

'A mother's love for her child is like nothing else in the world. It knows no law, it knows no pity. It dares all things and crushes down remorselessly all that stands in its path'

Witton Rehearsal

Unity moved into a building at the rear of the old bakery shop just opposite the junction on Prestbury Road. The owner was a black man called Duggie who only used the downstairs of the bakery. Therefore, we were able to rent the upper floor of the building and moved into it.

Access to the building was through a large drive which a van could easily be driven down to load equipment. This was great! Our first proper rehearsal room and Abbu's dad would no longer be nicking our stuff to do his gigs, or using it for his band rehearsals. Our new 'gaffe' was simply wicked! There was a large room with lots of windows and a small room which was the furthest away from the entrance door. The plan was that the small room would be used as an office whilst the band would rehearse in the large room. There were ample electric points positioned half way up each wall as it had been previously used as a sewing factory and shop.

Once we moved in, the drums took up the major portion of room; the keyboard section also occupied a lot of the space with the guitarists fitting in around the room with the vocalists in the middle. The microphone stands were littered everywhere with a large number of wires which were always a risk to the members who preferred to dance around whilst performing. We had loads of laughs in that rehearsal room and we spent many hours in there rehearsing and chilling. Naturally, rehearsal became a daily event and would last for many hours.

In order to improve my keyboard skills, it was necessary for me to submerge myself in a period of researching a wide range of artists. This enabled me to learn how other artists constructed their material. A variety of instruments were utilised in our music so that we could get that 'almost studio' sound. The keyboard section performed a variety of roles within the compositions by using the piano, organ and synthesizers. The piano would be used to co-ordinate song modification in the arrangement and I would often work on song parts with band members. The piano keyboard would be used as an accompaniment to assist the other band members in getting their parts right. The Hammond C3 organ was used to produce interesting chords and runs to get the best out of the 'Leslie' (a combined amplifier and two-way loudspeaker) which was a fundamental part of the band's sound. The Synthesizers enabled me to produce orchestral sounds that created chord runs and other dynamic sounds, able to compete with the solo pieces from the electric guitar.

However, the main problem was getting the organ to and from every gig safely. It was a major logistical problem normally involving a minimum of four people, including the two strongest who were Paul and myself, with help from any other person in the vicinity at the time. It weighed an absolute ton, literally, and between us we lifted that sucker all over the country and never dropped it once. The biggest problem was always getting it in and out of the practice room itself. Our rehearsal room was on the first floor and accessed via a wooden staircase that ran alongside the building. Everything else went up easily but a Hammond C3 organ ain't everything else.

It became clear that Ivor was struggling to make his percussion fit in with the new sound and his appearances at practice began to wane. If he did attend, he would only be socialising with the visitors who came to rehearsal. His percussion section was located closest to the door and all the visitors would end up talking to him and ultimately telling him to build a spliff - he was never ever too busy for that! Ivor saw his contribution to actual performances as minimal and always had time off for one reason or another. On one occasion, the band agreed to arrive early to rehearsal. Ivor didn't show up, which was strange as we rehearsed at the bottom of his garden. Someone went around to his house and Ivor eventually came to the door and explained that he had come to rehearsal, albeit slightly late. He said that he 'knew' he was going to get cussed, so decided to go home to console himself by smoking weed. I am sure you can imagine the response of the rest of the group on hearing this.

The Prodigal Son

Lloyd is a natural born singer and as his techniques

and abilities improved, he grew to become a great singer. His enthusiasm and creativity were always apparent and he got involved in every aspect of the band's music making. There were many occasions when we found him at practice early in the morning, sitting at the keyboards playing a tune or writing a song. Without doubt, Lloyd instigated a lot of the music with his basic chords and melodies. In the spirit of brotherliness, both Lloyd and I created the musical arrangements and Lloyd created the song melody around his lyrics. So it came as a shock when he made the decision to leave the band. The real reasons why he left the band have always been a mystery to me. Perhaps he was experiencing problems, or simply fed up of hours wasted in the rehearsal room repeatedly playing the same voiceless songs.

Technology - Synthesizers

Whilst working in engineering as an apprentice, I invested my wages in the latest keyboard equipment for myself. To achieve this, I had to ask my parents again to guarantee the finance for me. My purchases were a home stereo system to go with the boxes that Joey had made for me, the Yamaha DX7 synthesizer, Prophet 5 polyphonic Keyboard synthesizers and a Yamaha CX5 computer with Roland TR 606 Drumatix analogue drum machine. Upgrading to an Atari computer made it possible for me to connect the synthesizers and drum machine through the MIDI system.

Sitting on the Dock of the Bay (Watching the Crowd Go by)

Unity became renowned in the Birmingham music community and many artists who came to Birmingham hired our equipment to play gigs around the city. For example, when Maxi Priest's career as a singer began to take off, he came to Birmingham to perform and his management team contacted us to hire our equipment for the gig. A local promoter called 'Buff' aka 'Massive' RIP and 'Bigga Ford' brought Maxi to Birmingham. He was a singer on a sound system in London and had just made a single which had launched his career as a singer. However, his band were a bunch of opportunistic thieves and we realised that they had tried to steal my keyboards synthesisers. We had to chase the coach and flag it down so that we could jump on board to recover the equipment.

We were working hard and all we could see were other artists breaking through the barriers and achieving success. For example, Musical Youth, a group from Nechells in Birmingham, made a single which was a cover version of the Mighty Diamonds' track called *Pass the Dutchie*. Tony, the manager of the band, was around us on a regular basis and it wasn't long before they too were enjoying the life of success after their debut single went to number one in the pop charts.

UB40 Tour

In 1979, we supported the UB40 tour at the Derby Assembly Rooms. Paul managed to develop a relationship with the members of UB40 and visited them at their homes – performing at a UB40 gig is the equivalent of being with Kendrick Lamar today.

UB40 were the most generous people you could ever meet and Brian, the saxophonist, had an outstanding personality. Brian was in our changing room all day, giving us dope to smoke. At one point we went into their changing room where they were all building up from a big bag of weed. Someone then pulled out a massive bong and blazed it up and started to pass it around. Eventually it came to me, so like a trooper, I manned up and inhaled on the bong and continued inhaling until someone took it from me. After trying to exhale, the smoke wouldn't come out but maintaining a calm exterior, I was eventually able to blow the smoke out through every crack and crevice in my body. Standing there with my head aloft and my nostrils flaring as the smoke poured out of me and all I remember was feeling 'G-force' whilst falling backwards onto the floor. I was completely mashed and I blacked out.

It wasn't long until show time but we were all stoned. How we made it onto the stage is a mystery to me but we did and we were ready to perform! We did all the usual checks and had eye contact with each other so that we could start the first song after Lloyd's introduction. The crowd erupted and it seemed like all was well - Lloyd was jumping around the stage, belting out his dulcet tones. The song sounded great to me and the whole crowd were rocking. Lloyd, Ivor, Tracey, Danny and Abbu were jumping and skanking at the front of the stage throughout the whole song.

At some stage in the proceedings, it occurred to me that the drumming was far too loud and I couldn't actually hear my keyboards. Normally after the soundcheck on a gig, the engineers take control of the sound output and there is no need for adjustments to be made whilst a band is on stage. A musician knows that once the equipment has been set up after a sound check, you don't need to adjust the volume from the instrument itself. However, when you're playing a gig with a big band your equipment gets disconnected.

Lloyd's vocals ripped through the crowd and they were enjoying the opening number. I stepped back from the keyboards, jumping around like everyone else, I noticed that there were no lights showing on the keyboards. I pressed the keys and heard nothing and then the penny dropped. The keyboards were not even turned on! I was so stoned that I hadn't bothered to turn on the power to the keyboards and realised that the rest of the group must have been stoned too because none of the other instruments were playing. The only sounds coming out of the PA were the drum kit, congas, and the vocals.

I nearly died with embarrassment! The whole song had been performed before any of us started playing our instruments. The crowd thought that was the actual song and loved it, giving rapturous applause at the end. From that point forward we killed the show.

The lesson we learnt about performance is that if it doesn't kill you - it will make you stronger. One more thing to note is never smoke with the main act, because you only mess up your own performance.

Eclipse Band

Although I had heard all about the Eclipse Band, I never saw them perform. One day Tracey suggested that we go to Eclipse's practice that evening. Tracey didn't know exactly where their rehearsal room was, so we simply parked and hoped to hear the sound of music coming from somewhere. We headed towards a pub and could hear a voice singing in the distance; it sounded beautiful.

A stairway led to the room in which Eclipse were rehearsing. I was at the rear of the group, so as the door opened ahead of me the sound came blaring out and it sounded phenomenal. Upon entering the room we could see Eclipse in all their glory. The keyboard player had a Hammond organ with a little black electric keyboard on which he was playing the wickedest skank. The bass player had a Rickenbacker bass guitar and played a bass that was as smooth as silk. On the drums was the most violent drummer we had seen. He was beating his drum kit to death! His head was turning from side to side as he smashed the drumsticks into the skins as if to burst them with each stroke. In fact, he was just like Animal from the Muppet's Show band. On guitar was a dread playing a blend of jazz rock licks and the rhythm guitarist had a burgundy Gibson guitar. He just sat in the hole with the rhythm section. The vocalists were in fine voice and the harmonies were something else compared to our efforts.

Eventually, the number they were practising came to an end and we burst into spontaneous applause. They all stopped for a break and to hail up Tracey, many of them knew Pato's little brother and had heard from Pato that Tracey was now in a band. They extended a welcome to us all and made us feel at ease. All of them were really good musicians and the music sounded almost like a recording

I wandered over to the keyboard player, introduced myself and told him how good his technique was. He laughed and commented on my physical size and stature shouting to his brother "His name suits him, it's Hulk!" Everyone started laughing, whilst grabbing my hand to 'firm' me up. His tag was 'Brush' so maybe his name was Basil.

I had heard Hammonds used at church for years but not in a reggae context. I loved the whole keyboard sound. I always stuck to the factory setting on mine and none of those settings sounded like Brush's keyboard. The drummer, Derek, was the brother of the keyboard player and their family resemblance was strong with a distinctive but similar beard shape. The Bass player Didi soon caught my attention whilst talking to Abbu; he was a cool guy. The guitarist Nigel was a majestic figure but even then we sensed that he was bit more distant than the others. Tracey's brother Pato was one of the singers along with Jacko and Freddie the guitarist. Together, they produced a sweet sound, unlike any harmonies I'd heard before. Eclipse were leagues ahead of anything Unity had managed to create to date. Over the coming weeks and months, I regularly attended their rehearsals trying to learn as much as possible, particularly from 'Brush' the keyboard player.

There was a strange phenomenon amongst the Eclipse band that started before we came on the scene. Apparently one former band member, for no apparent reason, developed serious mental health problems on tour and within a matter of months, both the bass player Didi and then Didi's replacement became affected in the same way on tour. Fate seemed to have dealt a low blow but both the keyboard player and drummer began to experience the same issues. In the end, it seemed as though those not affected were truly survivors.

For years, all we ever heard about were the exploits of Eclipse and how Unity was rubbish compared to Eclipse. The mighty Eclipse band produced one album before health issues decimated the lives of most of their members. But their real achievement was that despite their difficulties, these guys stuck together to the end.

Cornerstone

In exactly the same way as the Unity crew went out together, so did other groups. We were able to meet and greet artists and promoters and find out about each other's gigs and schedules as well as organising visits to see bands at their practice sessions. Groups like Cornerstone, African Star and Black Symbol were all top Handsworth bands, so it was common to bump into them and to seize the opportunity to exchange information. These guys also had what sounded like quite a unique sound; they were strictly roots but their style of roots was distinctive. Cornerstone were absolutely rock solid, never missing a beat but the whole sound slowed as if it was being played in slow motion. Mr Brown dominated the stage and filled the room with his unique tones singing "sweet, sweet melody." The percussion section was always large and in charge with Benny aka 'Boot' who just sat in the hole with the deep roots bass. Drummy Conrad Kelly held that slow penetrating one drop as steady as a rock. Inspirational always.

Plan of Action - Rudimental Awakening

I and a few other band members enrolled at Solihull College on a GSE music course. We quickly realised that many of the people on the course, who were also musicians, were very mild mannered people and most of the time they were in awe of us as a band.

They thought that we were already professionals as their ambitions to date had only taken them as far as the course. Many were classically trained and could perfectly read music perfectly but they did not have the ability to jam. We, of course, were jam specialists. They said that my piano style sounded very 'jazzish'. On the whole, the course was a good experience and benefited us greatly.

1981. The First Prince's Trust Gala

Paul, our manager, became aware from the newspapers of a music competition with two thousand pounds prize money, which went a long way in 1980. It seemed easy, as we didn't have to audition; all we had to do was send a copy of a labelled demo cassette tape. Prior to this, we had never entered a formal competition and other than the initial discussion, before sending off the tape, the competition was never mentioned again.

It was just another normal day at the office in that we were at rehearsal, doing what sounded like our best to make the loudest racket possible in the name of music. Then the day changed from normal to thrilling when Paul told us that The Prince's Trust had contacted him to inform him that out of all the entries submitted nationwide, Unity had been selected by Prince Charles as the winner of their National Music Competition. The Prince was asked to choose an act from a plethora of shortlisted demo tapes. Apparently, he had met Bob Marley who performed at a concert in Africa in the same year. When he returned to England, he was on a high about the power of reggae music and rather than choose a rock or new wave band, he chose Unity because he was stilling feeling the vibe from his experience.

After hearing this news there was complete pandemonium – we were all elated. As Bob Marley said: *"When the music hits you, you feel no pain."* So clearly, Prince Charles had heard our drum and bass, and he felt no pain.

The prize was a show at the Dominion Theatre in London in front of Prince Charles. We travelled down in the van and did the soundcheck stuff. David 'Kid' Jenson, a popular Radio One DJ, came backstage, introduced himself to us and talked about the timing and introduction of the band. After performing three numbers, David would come back on stage and introduce the Prince who would make his way to the stage. We were expected to stand patiently on the stage and wait for the Prince to be introduced to us and then make his speech before returning to his seat to watch the remainder of the show. There were lots of different acts on the bill that day including Joan Armatrading and Phil Collins but none of that really mattered as the whole purpose of the celebration was to shine a light on us and the work of the Prince's new charity.

We were aware that there was a reception after the event at which the Prince would meet the winners for a chat offstage. There was a gentleman who worked for the Prince's Trust who should have been looking after us for the day. However, we soundchecked, did all the necessary photo shoots with the various papers and magazines covering the event, and did the performance. We met the Prince on stage, chilled with some of the big 'dappers' at the gig, packed up and left town at the end It wasn't too much of a task to drop everybody off home as the adrenaline rush meant that we were well 'hyper' anyway.

At rehearsal the following day, Paul came into the room shouting out expletives. He showed us the headline in a newspaper which read *"Rastas snub the Prince."* The paper got passed around the band as we all needed to see it to believe it. Questions, such as 'What do they mean?' were directed at Paul and he set about explaining his theory to us. The Prince's Trust man, the one who was supposed to be looking after us, had set us up and given the tickets, meant for the winning act to meet the Prince, to his own people. They pretended that we were not bothered about attending the reception with the Prince.

Suddenly, it was not just Unity, but our 'snubbing' of the Prince, the heir to the throne of England, meant that all Rastas had snubbed the Prince. Paul immediately contacted the Prince's Trust organisation on the phone and was furious with them. Apologies were flying both ways and everyone was made to look bad - both the organisation and the band. Of course, we contacted the papers with the true story but to them, it was not newsworthy.

Pato from Eclipse joined the Unity Management Team. This was a brilliant strategic move at the time as he brought experience and had a plethora of contacts for us to access for our benefit. Pato was already a respected part of the wider Unity family. His role was not intended to be musical or to contribute to the development of music or material within the band however, the opposite was accomplished. Over the two years, the guitarists had evolved and could certainly crank their guitars. They were now able to play a more significant role, rather than just some dreads picking a second bass or contributing tacky lead solos.

Over a period of time Tracey became the main lyricist for the band, primarily, because he always seemed to have some lyrics prepared in advance. The complacency of some band members resulted in a general apathy and apart from playing their own musical instrument, they made no further contribution. These guys simply refused to do anything that was outside of their comfort zone and it appeared that they did not take any responsibility for themselves in making their own way in business. In fact, the only time that any of the other five were prepared to put pen to paper was when they were signing recording contracts.

As only four people ever attempted to put pen to paper, I have to give credit where credit is due and it is fair to say that Tracey stepped up to the song writing plate when it was necessary. Although we didn't like or understand the lyrics, at least he put lyrics on the table to start the ball rolling with new songs. Quite soon any musical composition created in rehearsal resulted in Lloyd creating a song from Tracey's writings. Lloyd had an incredible ability to construct songs from any written words. This guy would literally pick up a newspaper and sing the stories out - a truly amazing talent to have.

Only four of the nine band members had ever put pen to paper or even attempted to write a song. In fact, the only time any of the other five were prepared to put pen to paper, was to sign recording contracts. Early on, it was clear to see that Tracey was extremely eager to contribute his lyrics to our music and, yes, it certainly helped us. He's a smart guy and realised that by consistently providing input, he would be in a better position to grab the 'lion's share' of any proceeds should the band ever achieve success.

As the band developed musically, Tracey became more verbose and dictatorial in the rehearsal room. Eventually he stifled creativity and new musical development by constantly rehashing old tracks. For years Lloyd persevered and made Tracey's lyrics into songs although the best of them had long since been used. Eventually we were singing songs that did not make any sense to anyone as the lyrics were self-indulgent and quite forgettable. This was the making of the straw that would eventually break the camel's back.

Post Prince's Trust

Following the Prince's Trust fiasco, Paul negotiated hard to ensure that the band still got the full prize for winning and insisted on the chance to record an album. This was subject to the approval of the company's producer. The plan was for the producer to come and see us rehearse to get the vibe of our music and then work with us in the studio to maximise the chance of success. Hey who cared? If successful we would be using one of the top studios in the country at the time. I suppose that was the moment some people thought we had made it.

The record company's A&R man was due to arrive the following Monday morning. It was at this point that Tracey declared to the group that as the lyricist, and regardless of contributions, all the songs technically belonged to him thus claiming the band's entire song collection. He went on to say that some of the songs were the property of his brother and so he too would claim ownership of any such material.

We were being 'jacked' and we didn't even have a record deal yet! This action totally shocked everyone to the core - particularly as Rastafari do not rob and steal, let alone from one another.

"There is no doubt that the negro is his own greatest enemy. He is jealous of himself envious and covetous, this accounts for most of our failure in business and other things." **Marcus Garvey**

At that very moment my fundamental beliefs in friendship and trusting fellow men were ruined and replaced with contempt. The collective unity that initially attracted me to join the band in the first place was gone forever. The problem was that it is impossible to 'un-ring' the bell once it has been rung.

Way back in the days of the honourable Harriet Tubman's struggle, such a man would have been shot. You see, one can't be slave and slave master, the oppressed and the oppressor, victim and the victimiser or God and the Devil at the same time.

The Honourable Marcus Garvey told us *"There are many negroes amongst us who will not go back to Africa because they are useless here and would be just as useless there."*

On the Monday morning at rehearsal, the members were still recovering from the bombshell dropped on us by Tracey at the tail end of the previous week. John, the A&R man arrived promptly and after formalities, proposed that we present the music that we had ready for the performance and he would kick back and listen to each track. He made it clear that he would inform us of his final decision at the end of the week. We set to work performing song after song and over the course of the week John was able to hear all the music in our collection.

The band was well rehearsed so we turned out the songs one after another without any problems. Naturally, everyone was nervous so the first day of the audition was conducted in relative silence, or was it the fallout from betrayal that everyone felt and managed with the utmost dignity? I guess we will never know. Even now I don't understand why we even turned up to do the audition. It was probably because we had spent ten years of our life sharing a common purpose in making music for the band whilst one member was taking crafty counsel to cheat 'I an I'. We had all been used and there didn't seem to be a damn thing any of us could do about it.

On Thursday, the day before he was due to leave, John arrived at rehearsal and got straight to the business of notifying the band of his decision. He said he felt the music was okay but it was just 'album' music and there had to be at least one stand-out song that could be used as a single. He had not heard that one special song, in fact none of the songs were commercially viable and as such, he had decided **not to proceed** with the record deal. John emphatically rejected the songs, all containing Tracey's lyrics, with the proviso that if we produced anything else before his train left the following day, he would gladly hear it before returning to London. Personally, I was delighted with the outcome.

As Bob Marley said: *"Soon we'll find out who is the real revolutionary"*. Here everybody had exactly the same challenge. The sheep put their heads down and got about their usual business without undue concern and resigned them self to the position that we were powerless stupidly saying 'well what can we do about it now?'

Maybe it was John's intention all along to motivate the dreamers to dream a little more and knew that those who dared to dream and sacrifice ultimately succeed. So, that night I wrote two simple songs at home using my box guitar. Two songs were delivered with lyrics and a complete arrangement ready for the very next day.

The next day I was shocked but not surprised that none of the other band members came to rehearsal with anything to contribute, not a cluster of chords or even a note from the thirteen available - just the old Negro spiritual *"I ain't got anything, but I'm gonna get paid."* I showed Lloyd the lyrics to the song I had written and sang him the tune. As soon as he heard me, he was away, and as they say 'like a dog with a bone' he nailed it - it sounded great. The other members were keen and quickly tried out their proposed parts, except Tracey. Instead, when he arrived at rehearsal he quickly disrupted the attempts by the members to learn their parts in the new music I'd provided. The he wanted to rehash another ancient track from the archives with lyrics he had written. Most of these songs had previously been thrown out by us because we knew they were not good enough. They were largely forgotten and in any case they sounded exactly the same as the music we had already performed for John.

When John arrived at rehearsal Tracey pressed forward to present another old song containing his lyrics - which didn't impress John anymore than those presented already. For the last time John asked if there were any other songs and if so, could he hear them? Finally, I told him we had something else, something slightly different from those already performed. He agreed to hear the songs as they were.

Quite suddenly, Tracey who was sitting on his amplifier, rose from his slumber, hoisted his guitar under his armpit and walked off into the back office. Everyone was shocked at his behaviour and despite his absence from the performances, the rest of the band pulled together and performed both of the hastily arranged songs for John. At the end of the second song, the room fell silent as we waited for his verdict. Suddenly the office door flew open and in strode the 'main man' himself, Tracey, taking his seat on top of his amplifier. I wasn't really sure what he hoped to hear because we had failed with all the songs containing his lyrics forced on us and were now waiting on a verdict on compositions that he had no involvement with at all.

It seemed like minutes, but it was probably only a few seconds before John's head tilted back and we could see his face. He had a very stern expression and looked directly at me. Then his expression changed and with a broad smile on his face, he rose up and moved towards me with an outstretched hand. He grasped my hand firmly, shaking one hand frantically whilst patting me on the back with the other, saying: *"That was great stuff! I loved them... that's what I've been waiting to hear all week."*

The room erupted in joyous celebration with

Andrew throwing his drumsticks up into air extending his arms upwards in a victory salute. Abbu was actually smiling, revealing his ivory white teeth which beamed from the darkness of his silhouetted figure holding the bass. Danny and Lloyd were shaking hands; actually we all shook hands with one other – we were ecstatic. John seemed to step into the background for a moment and just looked on as we all celebrated our achievement. The office door flew open and Paul and Pato came out to share in the jubilation and celebratory mood in the room. For me, it was completely mind blowing.

I stood back and looked up to God and gave thanks. Suddenly, I felt almost winded. I stepped back from my keyboards and bent over, resting my hands on my knee caps, inhaling and exhaling slowly. What an emotional roller coaster ride! Almost a week previously, we were all hit with the prospect of being ripped off by our 'brother', and then when faced with failure and probably the collapse of the band, we all pulled together and brought it back from the brink of disaster. We turned it around with a last ditch attempt - all except Tracey.

The easiest way for me to explain the whole scenario is to liken it to a basketball match. The feeling when the band were given one more chance to come up with something different was like being two points down at the end of a basketball game and having to score nothing less than a three point shot. Performing the tracks was not dissimilar to the point in the game when the ball is released by the player with less than a hundredth of a second left on the clock. The 'end of game' horn is blown yet the ball is still in flight heading towards the ring, whilst the spectators look up in anticipation. We were like the spectators, apprehensively awaiting John's verdict and at the moment when time stands still and everything seems as if it were in slow motion, the ball rolls into the net and instantly you feeel emotions ranging from shock to exhilaration, excitement to relief. The very same feelings we band experienced when John finally said 'YES'! At last VICTORY!

Whilst the rest of the band where still elated and animated, Tracey was content to sit on his amplifier with his guitar still under his arm, looking rather glum. Was this not the moment that we had all worked for all these years? Maybe he wished that the floor would open and swallow him up because in my mind, a person with a conscience should have felt highly embarrassed if they had failed an attempted coup. But not Tracey. In true dictatorial fashion, I don't think it even occurred to him that what he did had been wrong in any way. Quite frankly, he should have been **SACKED** on the spot.

Recording the Album 'Heat Your Bodies Up'

The day arrived and we were finally at the studio with the great producer and we began to put down our individual parts of the tracks. We had rehearsed hard to ensure that we were able to get it right the first time or as close to that as was possible. Re-takes were few and far between.

At the end of the first day it was already clear that the tracks were not sounding exactly the way we had hoped they would when recorded. There were particular tracks like *Rastaman* or *Believe In Me* which hit the desired mark and the sense of pleasure could be seen on the faces of the members. Hearing all the tracks together, at the end of each day's recording session, was a high point. We were to have our own album pressed and in the shops and Unity group would enter into the music hall of fame to be acknowledged and honoured amongst those who contributed to the story of reggae music here in the United Kingdom.

Only God knew what would happen next but at the time, that didn't matter to us. Everyone was proud that Unity had arrived at the top table. If a video camera had been available to me at the time, I would have taken the opportunity to record a message to the former school headmistress who had predicted our imminent demise. But in hindsight, I suppose that's why it is said that: *'Those who can, do. Those who can't, teach'*.

THE EPILOGUE

THE GREAT SHOW

The Zenith Show

Remember this was the 1980s and there were no archetypal, dreadlocked, leather-wearing, head-banging bands anywhere. This was it, the biggest gig we had ever done. The show was a massive visual spectacle which incorporated a huge sound system, fabulous lighting and pyrotechnics rigs designed simply to blow people away and appeal instantly to black and white fans alike.

As soon as the minibus stopped outside the venue we each grabbed hold of our personal items and headed straight for the changing room. It felt like we were gladiators, walking into a Roman coliseum – the expectation was massive. The soundcheck was exciting and the anticipation and suspense mounted.

After throwing down our bags in the changing room, we each claimed a spot to chill out after the soundcheck and then made our way to the stage. Once we were on stage, we began to set up our own personal zone as occasionally the 'roadies' would get something wrong, for example placing the keyboards the wrong way round.

We spent a considerable amount of time getting used to the sounds blasting from the PA system as they bounced off the walls and Bunny, the sound engineer, endeavoured to get the sound just right for the venue. Paul could be seen scurrying around giving last minute orders to the venue staff and road crew alike.

A considerable amount of time was spent on drum tuning and the drum kit used as many as fifteen channels on the mixer board. Tracey and Danny dominated the soundcheck with endless tuning; testing effect pedals and guitars with stands to use during the performance. Lloyd and I were by the keyboards going through warm up vocal numbers. Finally, the soundcheck was over and there was now a four or five hour wait until we appeared on stage.

Show Time

The compere enthusiastically bounded onto the stage, boosting the audience's mood and introducing us. This was it, we were the main act and it was now show time!

As the houselights went down, the nervous energy and anticipation could be felt as each of us made our way to our respective instruments to conduct final checks in the darkness. We could hear the audience talking and see them peering into the darkness. The stage lights beamed into the faces of the audience so they could not see onstage, only our figures in silhouette.

Andrew clicked his drumsticks and counted in the

start of the first song which instantly kicked in with powerful drums and guitar solos lasting a whole minute. Lloyd ran out onto the stage and grabbed the microphone from its stand, then struck a pose by putting his foot up on the foldback speaker at the front of the stage. He then delivered a masterclass in singing, weaving his spell over the beckoning women at the very front of the stage. He belted out the lyrics and fans responded instantly to his flamboyant and entertaining style. The audience's hands shot straight up into the air and they began to sway and move to the music - Unity's music gave life.

From behind my keyboards at the back of the darkened stage, I could vaguely recognise some familiar faces in the crowd, particularly at the front. For the very first time the 'WAGs' attended and I could see that my girlfriend had found a good spot to stand and watch the show and saw her waving to me from the crowd. The distinctive voices of our regular supporters like Eton, 'Eastman', 'Skipper', 'Lion' and 'Plug' along with many others, could be heard as they expressed themselves boisterously in the audience whilst looking on proudly as they acknowledged what we had managed to achieve. A few parents had braved the journey on the organised coach to watch us perform live for the first time. I don't suppose it really mattered what we sounded like. They were truly proud.

The first song ended with a dramatic combination of music, lighting and pyrotechnics. Suddenly, the stage became fully lit accompanied by two large explosions to the left and right of the stage and an outpouring of smoke. The stage filled with a mystical red, gold and green glow and the backdrop of His Imperial Majesty, Emperor Haile Selassie, was illuminated above us as we held our poses and were finally seen by the audience for the very first time. There was absolute silence in the arena. Although the audience knew they were coming to watch a black band perform, they were completely stunned by what they saw before them. We could see the look on the faces of the people at the front of the audience as they tried to relate what they had heard, to what they could now see. The deafening silence turned to applause which in turn became frenzied applause and screams. This was the cue for the next song.

Lloyd continued singing and running athletically around the front of the stage with Danny and Tracey strutting back and forth from side to side posing with their guitars. Tracey's black guitar and Danny's yellow guitar gleamed in the light and what emanated from them was positively electric. The show was simply astounding, amazing, dazzling and 'brand new good for you'. Those who met us personally were stunned at hearing our choice of music and sound and those others who heard our music first were stunned when they saw us live at shows.

Unity went on to play music at various clubs and venues such as JB's, Dudley, West Midlands, Ronnie

Scott's, Camden, and Dingwalls Club. We toured Scotland including Inverness, Glenrothes, Aberdeen and Edinburgh. We performed at the Manchester Apollo Theatre, Notting Hill Carnival, Cambridge University, Cardiff University and also supported Hugh Masekela in London. Also The Dome and the Odeon in Birmingham, Plymouth University, Kingston University, Coventry University and other venues around Burton on Trent, Leicester University and Derby and many more venues across the country. In the eighties we made several TV appearances including Channel 4's *Smiley Culture Show* and even performed on the Central News.

It is quite clear, though, that even after a decade of making music and performing in a star spangled show for royalty, it has been easy for our achievements to be discarded, erased, swept away on the tides of time. We accomplished something special and memorable that culminated in winning the Prince's award, and believe it or not, the first Prince's Trust Music Gala was said to be an historic event. Unity contributed to that legacy along with winners that came after 1982. However, the Prince's Trust has omitted to acknowledge us since, thus excluding us from history.

We are the boys from Poverty Street and as Martin Luther King Junior said:

"We always remember most the ones that were silent the most."

Our friends will recall that a certain group of lads from their school had a dream and purpose that we followed through together. It should have been the best experience of our lives but instead, behind the fake smiles, bombastic recollection of enthusiastic performances and the glory won for those few moments, there lies a much deeper pain; the haunting memory of betrayal. No matter how uncomfortable it may be to those concerned, it doesn't make the incidents a less offensive experience or any less true.

Within a year of the band winning the Prince's Trust competition and securing the record deal, I made the decision to leave. My rationale was that the band was now at its maximum flying altitude and a lot of interest was being shown from the music industry's entrepreneurs and companies. However, the main reason for my decision was that I had become completely disillusioned by the fake attitude of would-be leaders in the band, and as our work became more recognised, the bigger the lie became.

One year on and I was still seething from Tracey's destructive actions in the lead-up to the record deal. However, what disturbed me the most was the management's complete failure to address the truth regarding Tracey's behaviour and the fact that they were also focussed on claiming kudos for making music; something that even up until this day they can't do. Clearly, everyone was comfortable knowing they would reap the benefit from income gained from 'Heat your Body Up' as opposed to the 'no income whatsoever' deal offered by Tracey. By the time we got to the studios it was obvious that the members of the group had forgotten the coup attempt and were actually 'living in the lie'. One by one I watched 'brothers' sell their souls to the devil. What bewildered me was the question: if such a small amount of success could birth so much greed and dishonesty, what would have happened if the single or album had become a chart success?

So that was it; one day it suddenly dawned on me that I no longer trusted any of these guys and no amount of time spent with them in gigs or rehearsals would ever restore that trust or dispel the feeling of betrayal.

I have continued to make music but in the band I left behind the real problem of those 'living in the lie' was that they had never actually written a song before at all. So after devoting nearly ten years of my early adult life to making music in Unity, it was time to leave.

Although I have had a lot of pain in my life, I'll never let it reach my soul. Living in peace without any negative energy surrounding me allowed me to remain humble, and become who I really am. Throughout it all, I have endured and kept smiling. So as an inspired composer, I discovered my own happiness, the thing that defines me most and needs no excuses or approval. There is nothing that can compare to feeling of being inspired through music. Despite all the difficulties, I arose and lived the dream. The pain motivated me and I continue to rise, and as Maya Angelou said "I rise, I rise, I rise!" - *so I ain't mad at ya!*

GLOSSARY OF TERMS USED

A

A me bring you in dis world, so a me a go tek yuh out - I brought you into this world, so I can take you out of it (the world).
A who dat? - Who is it?

B

Back home people dem time deh - Jamaican people, in the old days
Bagwash - Launderette
Big man dem - Older men/respected or revered businessmen in the black community
Big man ting - Grown up business
Big me up - To big up an individual - to demonstratively acknowledge a person after an achievement
Big tings - Good things, success
Brand new and good for you - new and exciting
Browning - A woman who has a fawny, light brown complexion

C

Chacha man - Asian man
Chill-lax - Take it easy, relax

D

Dappers - Celebrities, stars, famous people
Dat one deh, it sound like da bom - That one, sounds like the best one.
Dem -Them
Dem come fe look fe me - They came to visit me.
Dem nuh know nothing u-nuh - They don't know anything.
Dem wan fe buy - They want to buy
Den dem just - Then they
Dutty - Dirty

E

Enuh - You know or do you know?
Edu-tain - To educate and entertain yourself

F

Facety - Cheeky, mischievous
Free loader(s) - Person or people who take advantage of another person's kindness or willingness to perform a task

H

Hungry belly boys - A term used for boys desperate to date/go out with a girl/woman.

I

I gwain bust you ass/me a guh bruk you ass - I am going to smack you hard
If you can't hear, you must feel - If you don't listen, you will suffer the consequences

K

Kiss mi teeth – Kissing teeth is a sound made by sucking air through the teeth and is done to show frustration/anger/disappointment
Kotched - balancing

M

Mik-case an come, me a go give you sup'n fe cry fa - Hurry up, I am going to give you something to cry for

N

Nuff - A lot of

O

Off the Hook - Amazing, extraordinary

Over Bright - Experienced beyond a person's age, extremely confident, sassy

P

Passa-passa – Gossip
Poppy show - Fake
Pull up - (in sound system terms), rewind the track to the beginning

R

Red skinned - A black person with a fair toned complexion
Rush - To chase with intent

S

Same way - In the same way
Sciffle - The shortest hair cut possible

U

Unuh - All of you, when referring to a group
Unuh gwaan - All of you carry on (doing)

V

Vex - upset/angry

W

Wasteman - Useless man
When dem reach and can't member what you tell

dem - When they arrived (got to their destination) and couldn't remember what they were asked to do
When you beg smady fe do something fe you - When you ask someone to do a favour
Wutless cruff - Useless person with no ambition

Y

Yardies - Jamaican born men
You a cry, and you nuh get nuttun yet - You are crying and nothing has happened
You can't stop in yah wid dat deh dutty head enuh, you fava damn thief, come outta me yard - You can't stay in this house with that dirty hair (locs), you look like a thief, get out of my house
You nuh hear me tell you nuh fe listen to dat damn foolishness in yah? - Didn't you hear when I told you not to listen to that rubbish ('Rasta' music) in this house?
Your eyes are bigger than your belly - Greedy
Your eyes are too red - wanting something that someone else has for the sake of it, not because it is necessary

Unity on top

Birmingham group Unity has been The band, pictured, was originally formed with a £300 gift from trust funds.

The seven-man band from Lozells won a national music competition run by The Prince's Trust, which was judged by Prince Charles.

They met up with Hank Marvin and Bruce Welch, of the Shadows, to receive their first prize cheque for £2,000.

The band was originally formed with a £300 gift from trust funds.

EVENING MAIL, SATU...

Unity are a Royal success

Only a handful of rock groups have had a chance to play before Prince Charles, and most of them are world-famous names.

But Birmingham band Unity were invited to perform for him at the Dominion Theatre in London last year, before most of the world had ever heard of them.

by
JACKIE BAILEY

That was when they won a contest organised by the Prince's Trust, and landed themselves the Royal Highness they had a £3,000 cheque as a prize.

That gave a big boost to their morale of equipment, and just seven months later they had something else to celebrate.

They landed a long-sought after recording contract with Charisma Records, and now their first single Heal Your Bodies Up is due out on July 15, followed by a self-titled debut album in September.

Keyboard player Owen Brookeland said: "We've been working quite hard, and we all play a bit better than we did last year.

"The music has changed quite a lot too - it's still reggae-based, but it's much more compressed."

When the band was formed five years ago, when the members were still at school, they were playing more reggae.

There have been several changes of line up since. But with the help of their music teacher, who taught them to play and freed them their first fans, Unity have built up a strong local following.

Owen said: "Our next ambition is to be respected as good musicians, but not as reggae artists."

"Our singles are aimed at Top Of The Pops and we just want people to enjoy them.

"We are not a political band. We are Rastafarian, but it is a personal belief, not something we would want to put into the music.

"Meanwhile, Unity play the next three at the Mulberry Arts Centre in Cannon Hill Park on July 26.

UNITY

by ROGER
TRAPP

for seven members of the eighteen-rock group Unity are sitting around giving selves hefty pats on the nobody could really blame

a debut album put out and a promising regular airplay on Radio own, and their radio contract to be last summer's Prince's Trust of competition.

... except for a notably happier ... they do not appear to have scrap to success.

... still only eight hours a day, ... a practice room at ... in Road, Aston and have already ... enough material for a follow-up ... debut album.

... it is that Unity have put in more

... in struggling that they cannot get out of the halls.

In their manager Paul Bonecogh says: "We did everything the hard way - practising for long hours, gigging to pay the bills, and ...

"But we've kept doing it because we believe in our ability. We are trying to improve the standard of music, that's around at the moment.

More bands start out with similar ideals, but we manage to stick together this year this band managed enough takings a break.

Their Unity succeeded where others have failed, it practice due to their methods and the talents bands they're cash with the whole and the whole of the band's are ... put one another.

All the members of the band - singer Lloyd Perry, bass player Anthony In-James, guitarist Danny McRae and

Danny Brimingham, keyboard player Owen Brookeland, percussionist and ... Davic Bundle and drummer Andrew Griffiths - are aged 15 and they, to home.

They all went to Broadway School in the district and they spend all their time together.

That's why they call themselves Unity. All the songs are recorded at Unity, and each member of the band is responsible for his own expressions," says Paul.

They were well received wherever they played. But they didn't make any real progress until last year's ... was a most exciting performance; that was the Prince's Trust competition.

"A few months before the contest or ... really quick. We were still playing ... but nothing was happening,"he explained to the Birmingham branch at the time.

"We didn't have anything, man - until they told us in a letter saying they were having a competition.

"We're so really a band for that sort of thing. But we entered. There was about 25 or 30 others in the country. And we won," insists Paul.

They won a much revered £3,000 and Charisma gave them a cheque, then more importantly, the win in front of Prince Charles and led a career record.

It came from the Charisma ... company into hands, and something ... devoted to tape the seven Rastafarians from Aston.

With their run-out releases and a well-heralded local artist gear, Unity must look likely to be one of this year's more interesting bands.

PICTURE 1 _____Me shooting hoops, Hollyhead School 1985

PICTURE 2 _____The Raving Crew, Tabascos 1985

PICTURE 3 _____ Wedding Photo 1985

PICTURE 4 _____Aunt Lee, Summerfield Hospital 1960'S

PICTURE 5 _____Newspaper clipping

PICTURE 6 & 7 _____Me at Broadway Youth Club 1980/1981

PICTURE 8 _____Keith Copeland and 'Bigga Ford' 1980

PICTURES 9 & 10 _____Great Barr School Rugby Team 1973/1974

PICTURE 11 _____Newspaper clipping

PICTURE 12 _____ Newspaper clipping

PICTURE 13 _____Largie, George, Eton & Me 1978

PICTURE 14 _____Unity (back) Me (middle) Tracey & Lloyd (bottom) Ivor, Andrew, Danny & Abu 1980/1981

PICTURE 15 _____Great Barr Comprehensive School